# How the EARTH works

Dr. Lucía Pérez-Díaz

**Author and illustrator** Dr. Lucía Pérez-Díaz
**Consultant** Graeme Eagles

**Project Editor** Sophie Parkes
**Senior Art Editor** Laura Gardner
**Project Art Editor** Victoria Palastanga
**Managing Editor** Gemma Farr
**Managing Art Editor** Anna Hall
**Production Editor** Gillian Reid
**Production Controller** Leanne Burke

First published in Great Britain in 2025 by
Dorling Kindersley Limited
20 Vauxhall Bridge Road,
London SW1V 2SA

The authorised representative in the EEA is
Dorling Kindersley Verlag GmbH. Arnulfstr. 124,
80636 Munich, Germany

Text and illustration copyright © Dr. Lucía Pérez-Díaz 2025
Layout and design copyright © 2025 Dorling Kindersley Limited
A Penguin Random House Company
10 9 8 7 6 5 4 3 2 1
001–342077–Mar/2025

All rights reserved.
No part of this publication may be reproduced, stored in or
introduced into a retrieval system, or transmitted, in any form,
or by any means (electronic, mechanical, photocopying,
recording, or otherwise), without the prior written permission of
the copyright owner.

A CIP catalogue record for this book
is available from the British Library.
ISBN: 978-0-2416-8546-4

Printed and bound in China

www.dk.com

# CONTENTS

INTRODUCTION ......... 4

BEFORE WE BEGIN ......... 6

A LUCKY ROCK ......... 8

ALL WRAPPED UP ......... 10

FULL OF LIFE ......... 12

WELL-HIDDEN SECRETS ......... 14

A PUZZLING DISCOVERY ......... 16

THE ENIGMA CONTINUES ......... 18

MARIE'S MYSTERY MOUNTAINS ......... 20

JOINING THE DOTS ......... 22

A NEW THEORY IS BORN ......... 24

A LAYERED PLANET ......... 26

PLATE TECTONIC THEORY ......... 28

BIG... OR SMALL? ......... 30

ALWAYS IN MOTION ......... 32

COMING THROUGH! ......... 34

OPENING UP ......... 36

ONE BIG PUZZLE ......... 38

HISTORY REPEATING ......... 40

MAKING SPACE ......... 42

SINKING PLATES ......... 44

MORE SINKING PLATES ......... 46

CRUMPLING PLATES UP ......... 48

AN INTERCONNECTED SYSTEM ......... 50

WHAT DRIVES PLATE TECTONICS? ......... 52

ONE WORLD TODAY ......... 54

A DIFFERENT WORLD TOMORROW ......... 56

PUTTING THE PIECES TOGETHER ......... 58

THE SECRET INGREDIENT FOR LIFE ......... 60

THE CARBON CYCLE ......... 62

MOVING TOO FAST ......... 64

TIME TO ACT! ......... 66

NOT JUST OUR PLANET ......... 68

WORLDS TO DISCOVER ......... 70

A GROUP EFFORT ......... 72

THE NEXT CHAPTER ......... 74

GLOSSARY ......... 76

INDEX ......... 78

ACKNOWLEDGEMENTS ......... 80

# HOLA!

My name is Lucía, and I'm an Earth scientist. I investigate what our planet looked like in the past, and how that has shaped the world we live in today. But I have a little secret to share with you – I didn't always know I wanted to be a scientist. When I was your age, all I knew was that I loved solving puzzles, asking questions, and figuring out how things worked... I had no idea that that's exactly what science is all about!

In this book, I am going to take you on a grand adventure, deep into one of the most fascinating puzzles that I know of – our Earth! Did you know that Earth's surface is made up of enormous, shifting puzzle pieces? Their movements shape everything around us, from our towering mountains and deep oceans, to the existence of earthquakes and volcanoes, and even to the conditions that make life on our planet possible. The theory that explains all of this is called plate tectonics. I hope that, as you read, it inspires you to ask your own questions about the world around you – that's where the real fun begins!

Remember, every great scientist started out just like you – with a curious mind and a love of discovery. So who knows? Maybe one day you'll be the one solving some of the many remaining mysteries of our planet!

Lucía

# BEFORE WE BEGIN

Throughout this book, there are some really big numbers. When it comes to planet Earth, we need these numbers for a lot of things! Earth's size is measured in thousands of kilometres, and its age in millions, and sometimes even billions, of years. The best way to understand how big those numbers really are is to compare them to our own lives...

**EARTH'S CORE**
6,371,000 steps

### QUITE A LONG WALK
Take the distance between the surface and the very centre of Earth – around 6,371 km (3,959 miles). If you walked 10,000 steps a day, and taking into account that a person's step is about 1 m (3 ft) long, it would take you more than two years to get there!

### OLD OR YOUNG?
Numbers become even bigger when you think about our planet's age – 4.6 billion years. That is the same as 4,600 million years.

Humans have only been around for the last 2.9 million years of that.

However, Earth is pretty young if you compare it to the age of the Universe, which is almost three times older.

**HUMANS**
2.9 million years

**LIFE ON EARTH**
3,500 million years

**EARTH**
4,600 million years

**UNIVERSE**
13,800 million years

## A SPECIAL CALENDAR

Just like we use calendars to organise our lives and make notes of important events, Earth's life is recorded by Earth scientists in a very special kind of calendar – the geological timescale. And just as our calendar is divided into years, months, and weeks, geological time is divided into eons, eras, and periods.

Eons are the biggest division in the geological timescale – there are four of them.

**EONS**

**HADEAN**

4,000 MYA

Earth's formation: 4,600 MYA (million years ago)

First life forms (bacteria): around 4,000 to 3,500 MYA

**ARCHEAN**

The first three were rather quiet. Not that much happened for the whole first 4 billion years...

2,500 MYA

Unlike our calendars, the geological timescale is not divided into sections of equal length. Instead, the beginnings and ends of eons, eras, and periods are chosen at times when important things happened.

**PROTEROZOIC**

For example, the time when dinosaurs became extinct was chosen to mark the end of the Mesozoic Era, and the start of the Cenozoic Era, 66 million years ago.

In contrast, lots of important things happened during the eon we are in now – the Phanerozoic. That's why it is divided into smaller chunks called "eras". Eras are then divided into "periods".

541 MYA

**PHANEROZOIC**

TODAY

| ERAS | PERIODS | |
|---|---|---|
| Paleozoic | | — Fish |
| | | — Reptiles |
| Mesozoic | | — Mammals ⎫ Dinosaurs |
| | | — Birds ⎭ |
| Cenozoic | | — Humans |

7

# A LUCKY ROCK

Our Solar System is made up of of eight planets, hundreds of moons, and thousands of asteroids, all orbiting around one star: the Sun. Only one of these places is home to life today: Earth.

Neptune

Uranus

GAS GIANTS

Saturn

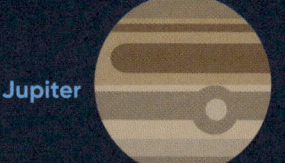
Jupiter

ROCKY PLANETS

THE SUN

## ROCKY PLANETS

Earth is a rocky planet, and so are Mercury, Venus, and Mars. Unlike the four gas giants, which are cold and inhospitable planets without solid surfaces, the rocky planets are made up of... well, rocks – and metals!

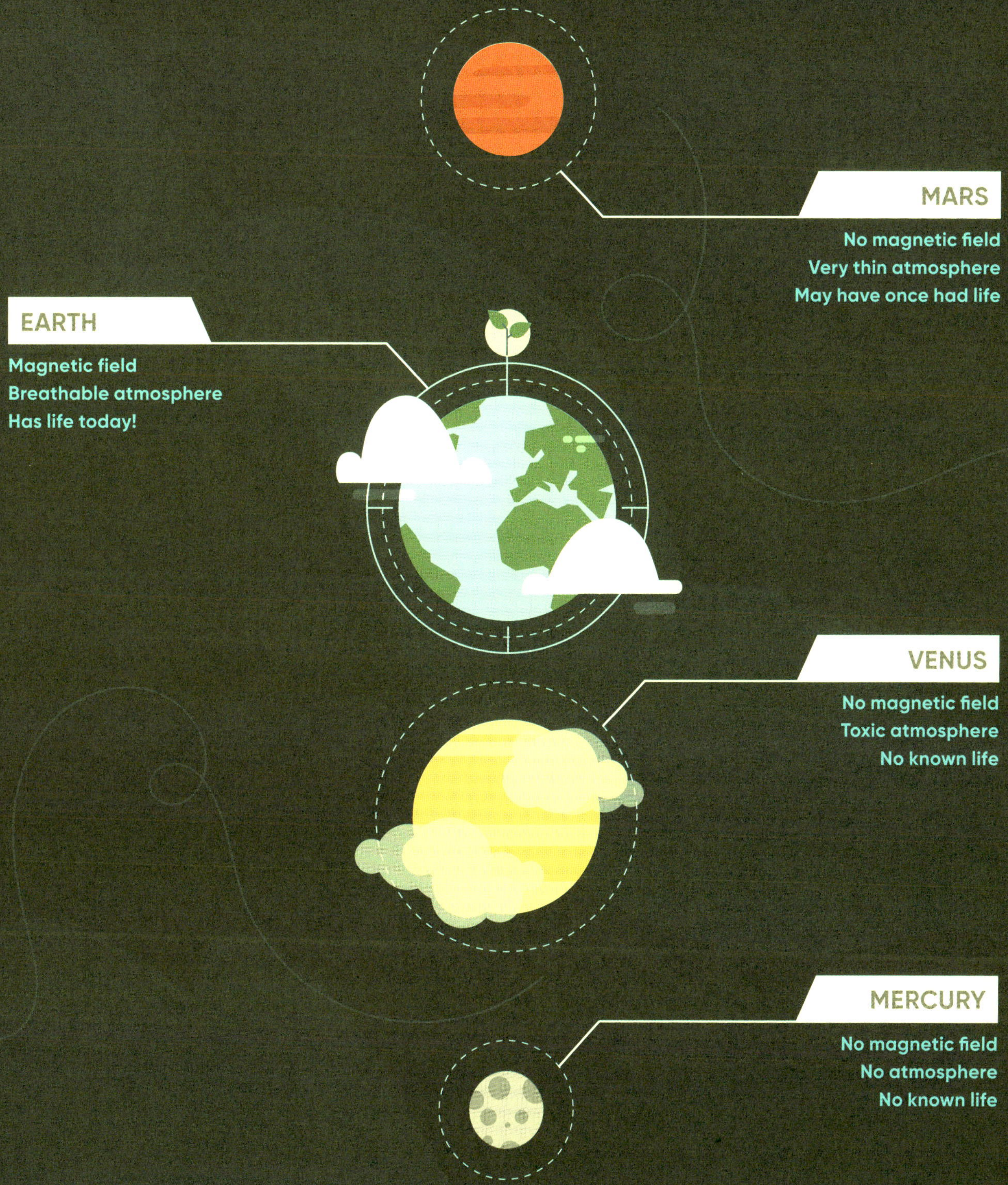

### MARS
No magnetic field
Very thin atmosphere
May have once had life

### EARTH
Magnetic field
Breathable atmosphere
Has life today!

### VENUS
No magnetic field
Toxic atmosphere
No known life

### MERCURY
No magnetic field
No atmosphere
No known life

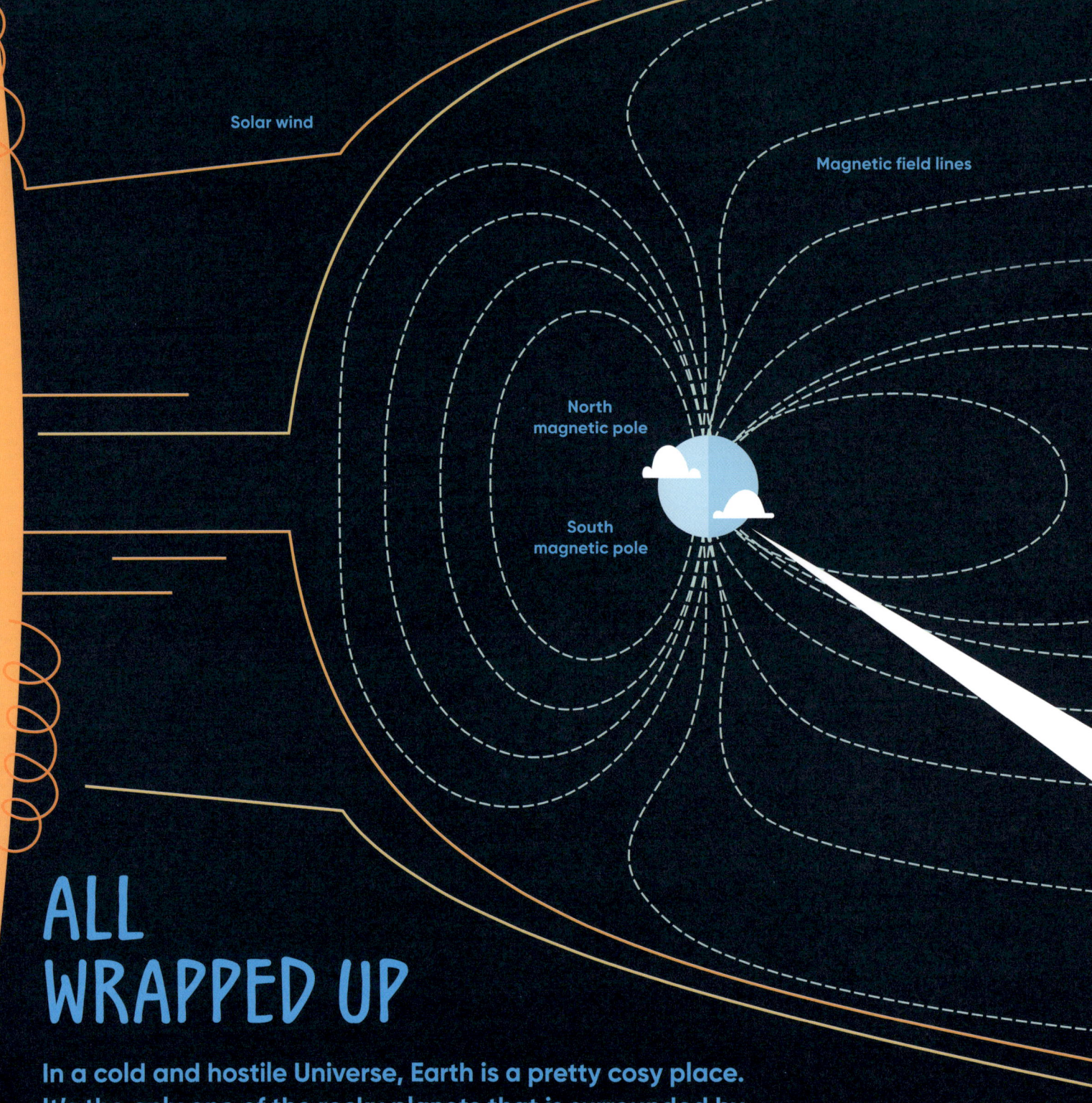

# ALL WRAPPED UP

**In a cold and hostile Universe, Earth is a pretty cosy place. It's the only one of the rocky planets that is surrounded by a strong magnetic field, which acts as a shield protecting it from dangerous cosmic radiation and solar winds.**

Earth's invisible magnetic field lines run in a loop, entering the planet through the north magnetic pole, and exiting at the south magnetic pole. They are pushed away strongly by solar wind, which squashes them on one side, and stretches them away from the planet on the other – a bit like the way that water is pushed by the front of a moving ship.

As well as being protected by this invisible magnetic armour, Earth is located in just the right place. It is far enough away from the Sun to not get too hot, but wrapped in a breathable atmosphere "blanket" that keeps it from becoming too cold.

These two invisible shields make Earth the only planet in the Solar System capable of sustaining life.

## EARTH'S ATMOSPHERE

Oxygen: 21%

Nitrogen: 78%

Argon: 0.9%

Carbon dioxide: 0.04%

Other gases: 0.06%

The boundary between Earth and space is called the Kármán line. It is only 100 km (62 miles) from Earth's surface. If you fly above it, you are a space traveller!

The atmosphere is around 1,000 km (600 miles) thick.

# FULL OF LIFE

With its magnificent mountains and deep oceans, rich rainforests and arid deserts, fresh water lakes and lush mangroves, Earth looks very different to the other rocky planets, doesn't it? Despite this, the rocky planets are all the same age – about 4 billion years old.

Hidden throughout Earth's landscapes are the clues telling us all we need to know about its life story. The detectives searching for these clues and putting them together are called Earth scientists.

Some decades ago, they discovered that Earth has a well-kept secret that not only explains why it is so different from its neighbours, but also might even be the reason we are all here today.

And it's happening **right beneath your feet...**

# WELL-HIDDEN SECRETS

The thing about secrets is... they are hard to figure out!
It's one thing to realize Earth is quite different from its
neighbours, but finding out why – that's trickier.
It all starts with a pretty simple question:

Has Earth always looked the way it does today?

At first, people assumed that continents and oceans
must be permanent features on Earth's surface, and
had not changed since Earth's life began. After all, how
could something as big as a continent possibly move?!

But as explorers started travelling the
world and drawing the first detailed maps
of our planet, they began to suspect that
things maybe weren't so simple...

# A PUZZLING DISCOVERY

Centuries ago, mapmakers noticed something curious about their maps. Some continents, although they were now great distances apart, looked like they once fitted together perfectly, like the pieces of a puzzle.
Could that have been the case?

Cynognathus, an extinct, mammal-like reptile (250-230 MYA)

Glossopteris, a woody seed plant (300-200 MYA)

Some time later, explorers found that the same rock types could be found on different continents far from each other. They even realized that those rocks contained fossils of the same plant and animal types.

Eventually, in 1912, scientific explorer Alfred Wegener put the puzzle pieces together. He came up with a theory called "continental drift", which suggested that, a long time ago, all the continents must have been part of a single supercontinent. Over time, it must have split into pieces that drifted across Earth's surface to the places where they are located today.

# THE ENIGMA CONTINUES

Although Alfred Wegener's theory of continental drift explained the observations at the time, he couldn't explain why this supercontinent would have broken into pieces, or how huge pieces of land could travel across great distances. Very few people took him seriously.

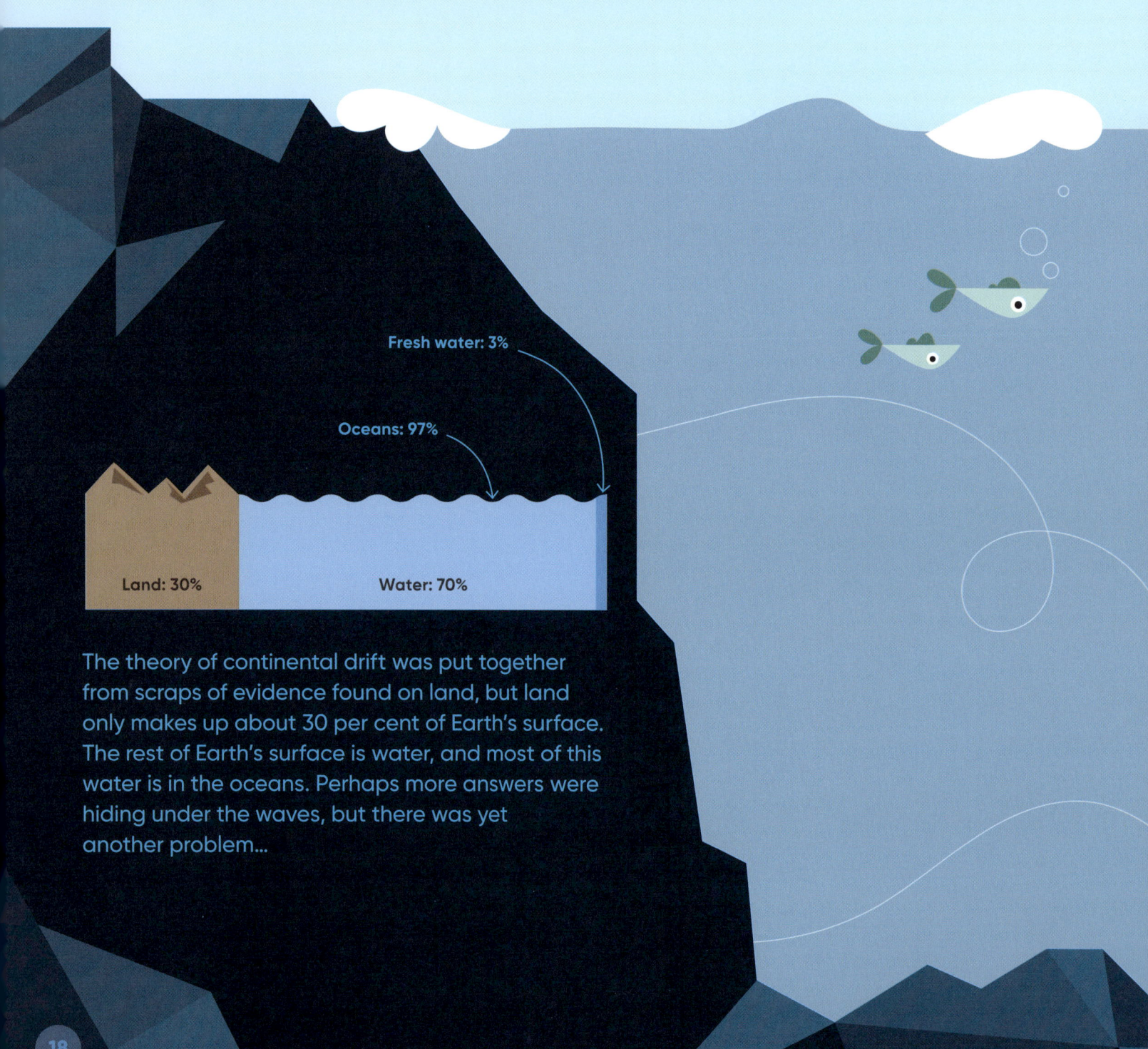

Fresh water: 3%

Oceans: 97%

Land: 30%  Water: 70%

The theory of continental drift was put together from scraps of evidence found on land, but land only makes up about 30 per cent of Earth's surface. The rest of Earth's surface is water, and most of this water is in the oceans. Perhaps more answers were hiding under the waves, but there was yet another problem...

In the early 20th century, when Wegener came up with his theory, oceans were a great big mystery. We had no idea about how deep oceans were, or how they may have formed or evolved.

This would change a few decades later, thanks to advances in technology and, in particular, the development of something called sonar.

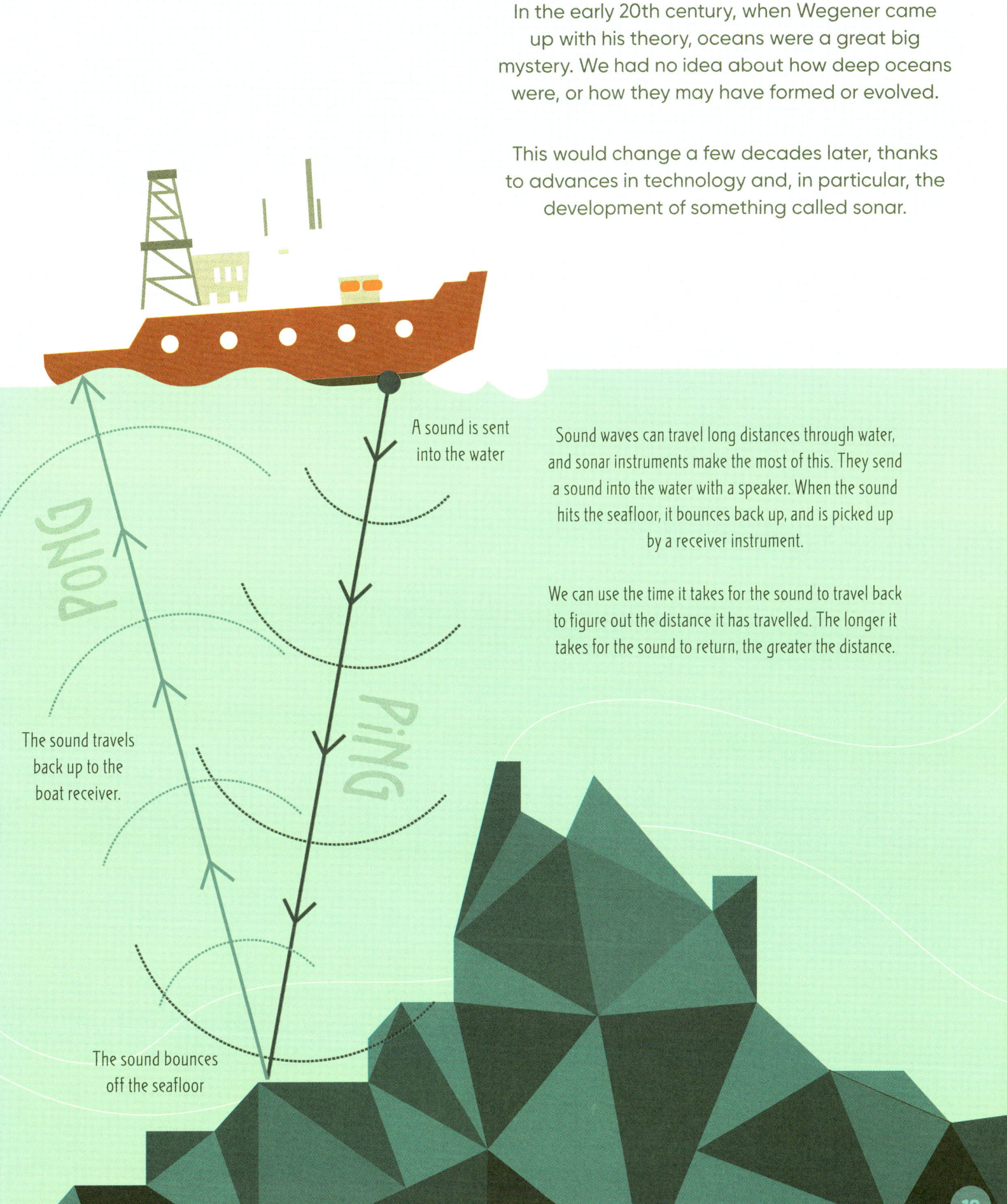

A sound is sent into the water

The sound travels back up to the boat receiver.

The sound bounces off the seafloor

Sound waves can travel long distances through water, and sonar instruments make the most of this. They send a sound into the water with a speaker. When the sound hits the seafloor, it bounces back up, and is picked up by a receiver instrument.

We can use the time it takes for the sound to travel back to figure out the distance it has travelled. The longer it takes for the sound to return, the greater the distance.

# MARIE'S MYSTERY MOUNTAINS

Many ocean expeditions during the 1950s and 1960s carried sonar equipment on their research ships. With this, they were able to start mapping large areas of previously unexplored ocean floor, such as in the Atlantic Ocean, between North America and Europe.

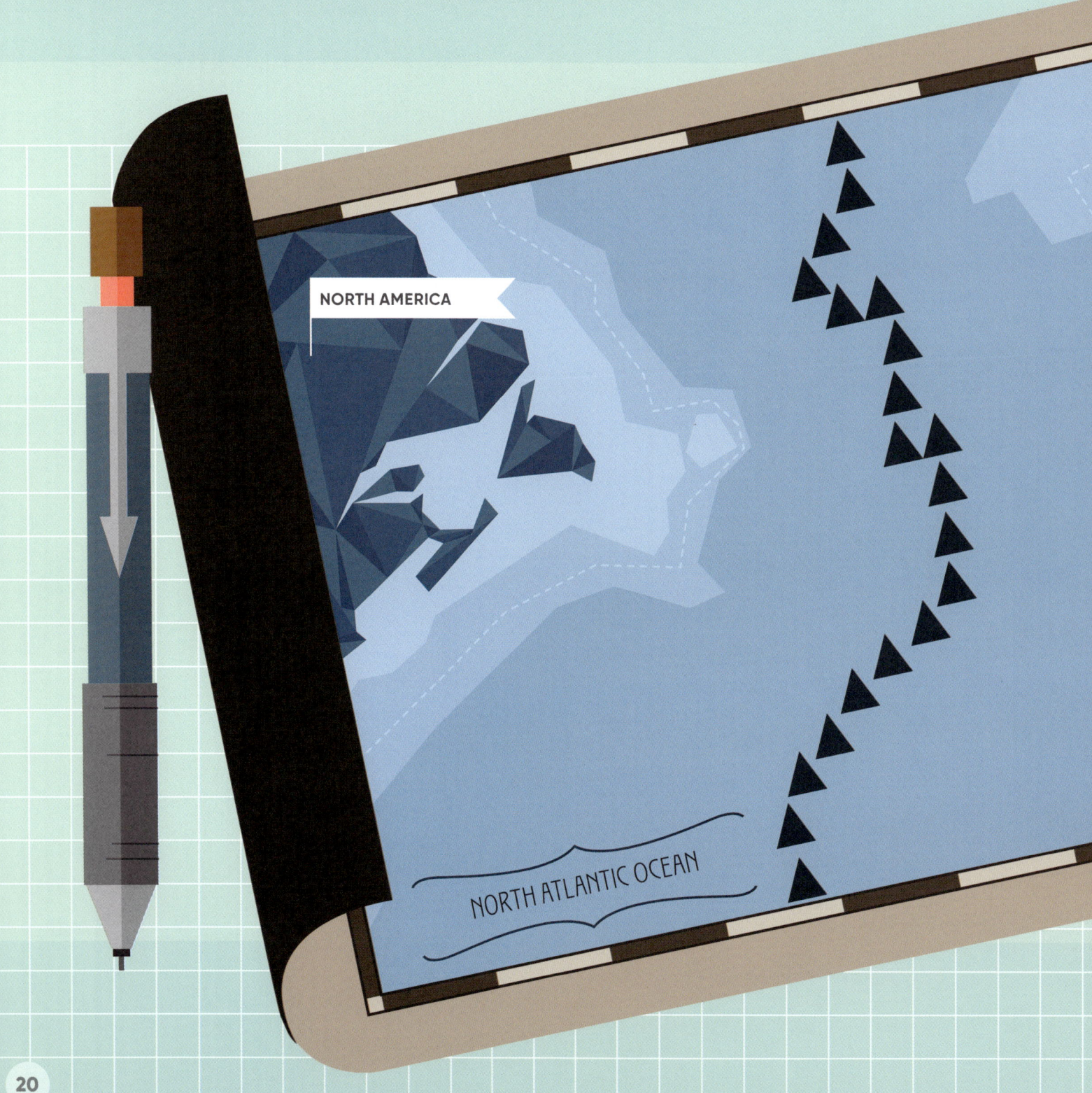

Marie Tharp, 1952

This led to one very unexpected discovery, made by a scientist called Marie Tharp. Marie was a cartographer – a person who draws maps. In 1952, using sonar measurements collected across the Atlantic Ocean by research expeditions, she started drawing the shape of the seafloor, and found that it wasn't flat. In fact, running through the middle of it was a chain of underwater mountains more than 2 km (1.2 miles) tall!

EUROPE

AFRICA

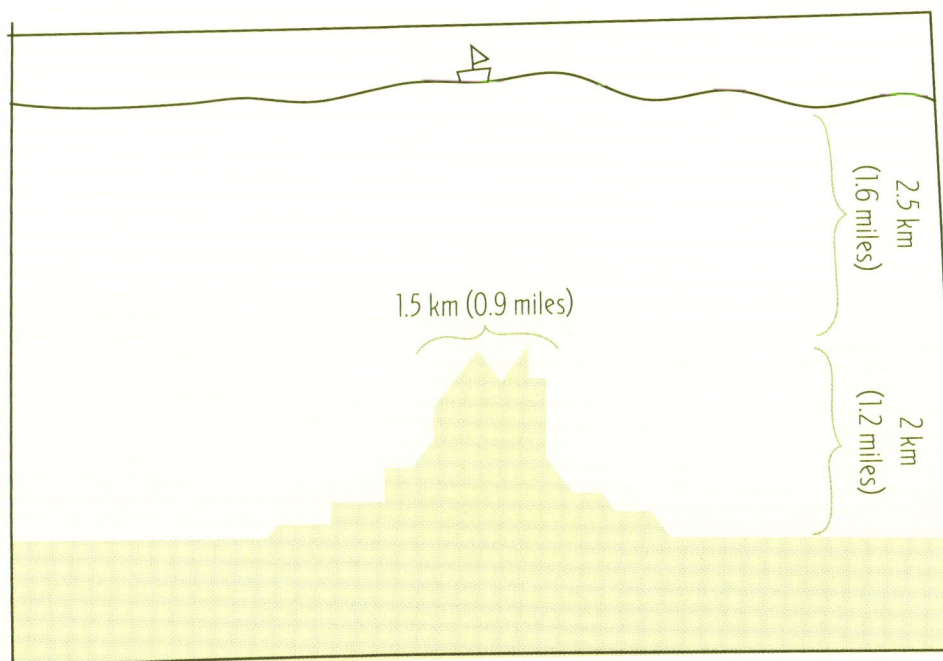

The discovery puzzled scientists, who couldn't quite explain why the mountains were there or how they formed.

Marie made her discovery before ever going on a research ship herself. This was because, at the time, many people still believed that it was "unlucky" to have women on ships, unless they were being carried as passengers. Marie was not able to join aboard on research expeditions until 1968.

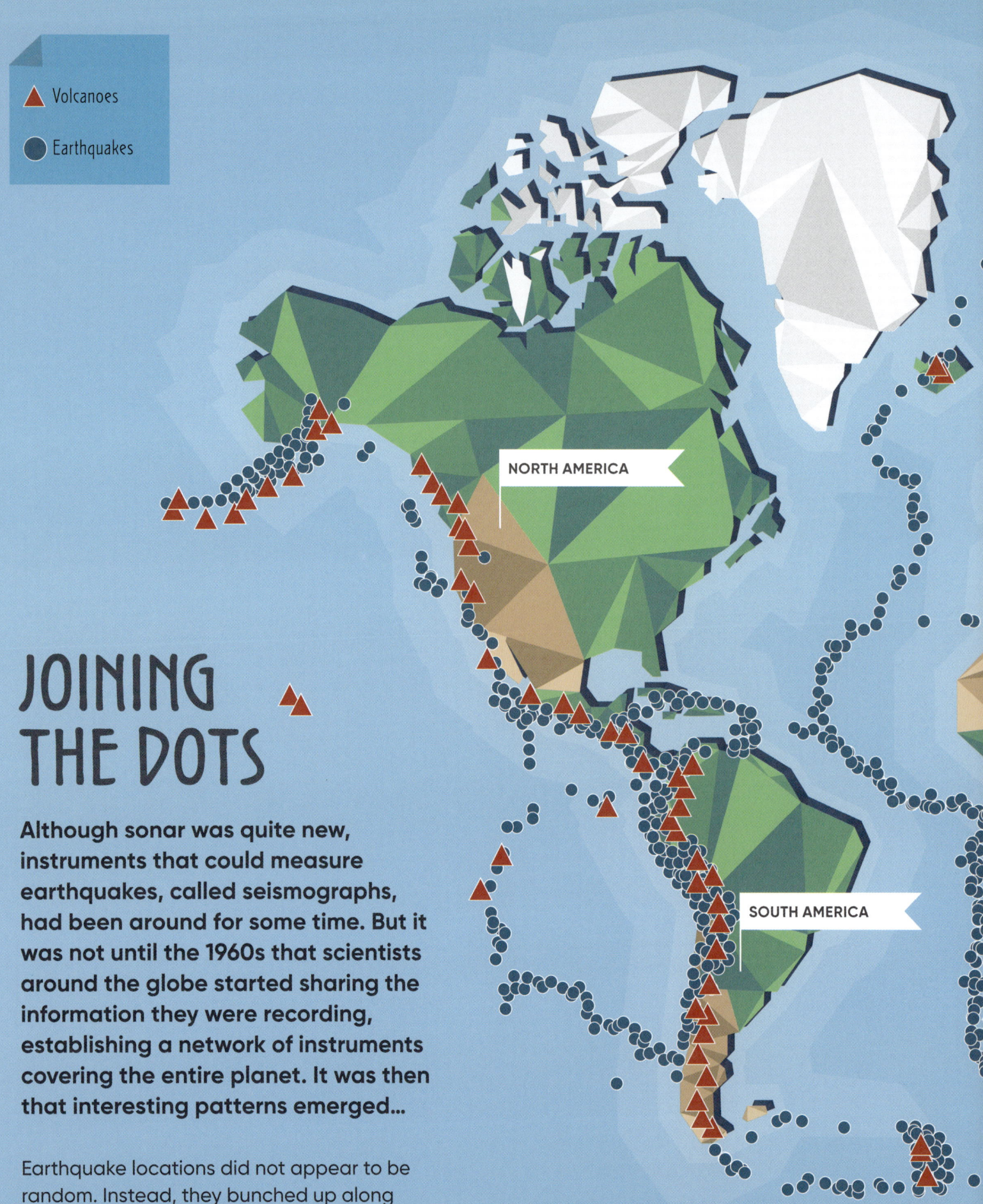

- ▲ Volcanoes
- ● Earthquakes

NORTH AMERICA

SOUTH AMERICA

# JOINING THE DOTS

Although sonar was quite new, instruments that could measure earthquakes, called seismographs, had been around for some time. But it was not until the 1960s that scientists around the globe started sharing the information they were recording, establishing a network of instruments covering the entire planet. It was then that interesting patterns emerged...

Earthquake locations did not appear to be random. Instead, they bunched up along specific zones of the planet.

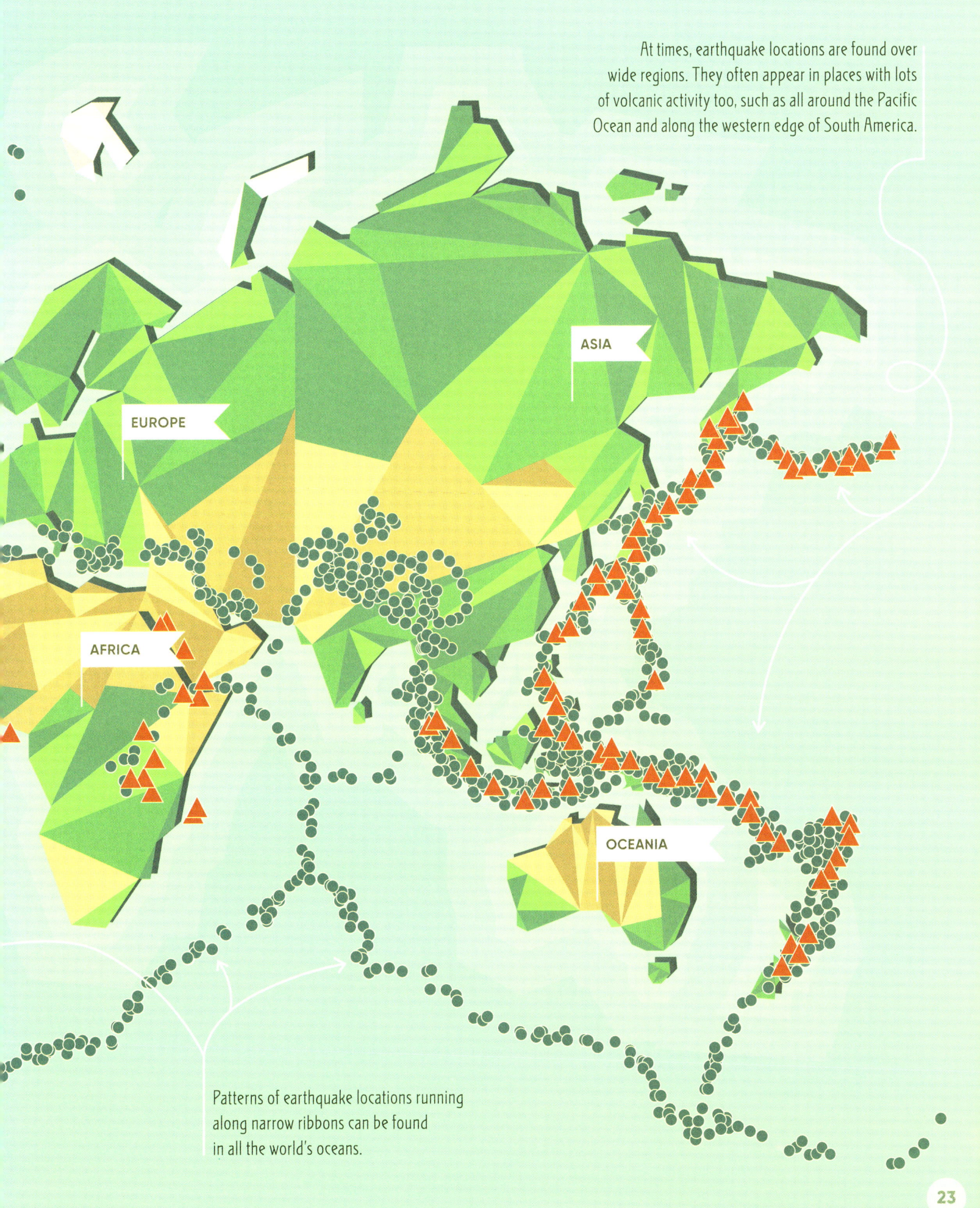

# A NEW THEORY IS BORN

All of these discoveries were like pieces of a jigsaw. By themselves, it was very hard to figure out what they meant, just like you can't tell from a single piece what a jigsaw will show when it's complete. However, if you look at all of the pieces together, you might just start to see the full picture...

By now, Earth scientists had quite a few pieces of the jigsaw.

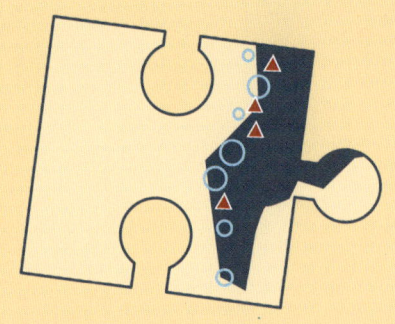

Earthquakes and volcanoes appeared only to group along certain regions of the planet – but why?

Some continents looked like they once fitted together, but how could a continent have broken apart?

There were mountain ranges right at the very bottom of oceans, where nobody expected to find them!

Eventually, they realized that the discoveries they had made could all be explained as the result of a very important process that happens on Earth, and only on Earth...

A new theory was born, and Earth scientists called it

## PLATE TECTONICS

# A LAYERED PLANET

To understand plate tectonics, you first need to understand what the inside of Earth looks like – it is a layered planet. If you drilled a hole down from the surface and towards the centre, you would first go through a thin crust, formed of various different rocks.

**CRUST**

There are two types of crust – oceanic, which is mostly a rock called basalt, and continental, which is mostly a rock called granite.

**ATMOSPHERE**

0 to 75 km (0 to 47 miles)

6,370 km (3,958 miles)

**MANTLE**

This layer is made up of peridotite rocks. Although it is solid, it can flow, but it does so very, very, VERY slowly.

2,900 km (1,802 miles) below the surface

**CORE**

This layer is made up of iron, nickel, and sulphur.

After that, a lot of your journey would be through a rock type called peridotite, which forms the mantle. However, that doesn't mean your journey would be boring! Despite being made of only one rock type, different regions of the mantle behave in different ways because they are under different temperature and pressure conditions.

Eventually, you would make it all the way to the core, which is made up of metals instead of rocks.

### LITHOSPHERE

This layer is made up of the crust and the very top part of the mantle. It behaves as a tough, rigid solid and is broken into pieces called tectonic plates.

### ASTHENOSPHERE

This layer is partly molten and can flow. It is part of the mantle where the temperature is between 1,300°C (2,372°F) and 1,700°C (3,092°F).

The depth at which the lithosphere and asthenosphere start and end is not fixed. Instead, they are thermal boundaries. This means they are located where a certain temperature is reached within the mantle.

1,300°C (2,372°F)
1,700°C (3,092°F)

### OUTER CORE

This layer is liquid.

### INNER CORE

This layer is solid.

At the centre of Earth, temperatures reach more than 5,000°C (9,000°F). That's as hot as the surface of the Sun!

# PLATE TECTONIC THEORY

The lithosphere (the outermost of Earth's layers, formed by the crust and the very top of the mantle) is broken up into several pieces, all of which move constantly by gliding over the soft, hot rocks of the asthenosphere (the layer beneath). Each of these pieces is called a tectonic plate, and they don't all look the same.

Some carry continents…

…and some don't.

Some are small…

...and some are big!

(And their shapes and sizes change over time.)

They don't all move at the same speed, but they do all move, all the time, and have done so for billions of years. Plate tectonic theory describes these movements, and how they impact the way Earth looks and works.

Right now, beneath your feet, is a tectonic plate, and it's taking you along on its journey.

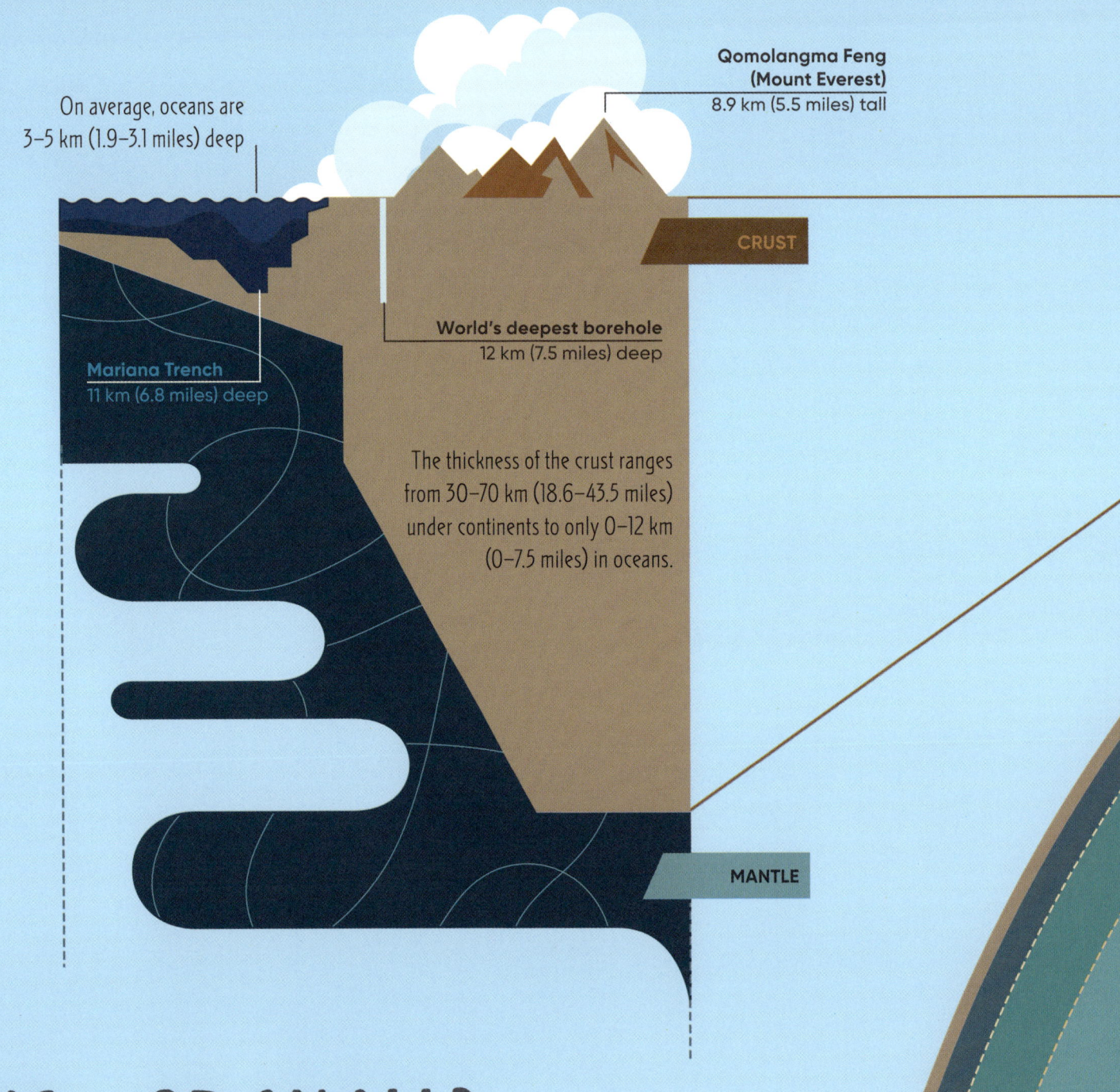

On average, oceans are 3–5 km (1.9–3.1 miles) deep

Qomolangma Feng (Mount Everest) 8.9 km (5.5 miles) tall

CRUST

World's deepest borehole 12 km (7.5 miles) deep

Mariana Trench 11 km (6.8 miles) deep

The thickness of the crust ranges from 30–70 km (18.6–43.5 miles) under continents to only 0–12 km (0–7.5 miles) in oceans.

MANTLE

# BIG... OR SMALL?

**The impressive depths of our oceans and the magnificent heights of our mountain ranges make us, standing here on the surface of Earth, feel like we are quite small in comparison. But, if you consider how big Earth is, even the tallest mountains become tiny compared to it!**

In fact, if Earth was the size of an apple, the crust – and all life as we know it – would be contained within the apple's skin!

Mountains, oceans, and all life as we know it are right here – on the very outer layer of Earth!

1,300°C (2,372°F)

1,700°C (3,092°F)

Tectonic plates are made out of lithosphere, which is formed from the crust and the very top part of the mantle. Like the asthenosphere, instead of being found at a particular depth, the bottom of the lithosphere is defined by temperature: where the mantle reaches 1,300°C (2,372°F).

The part of the mantle that tectonic plates glide over is called the asthenosphere. Its top and bottom are found at specific temperatures instead of depths: 1,300°C (2,372°F) and 1,700°C (3,092°F).

**MANTLE**  **CORE**

# ALWAYS IN MOTION

**On average, tectonic plates move about as fast as your fingernails grow.**

This might seem quite slow, and in fact most of us live our lives without ever noticing that we are on board a moving tectonic plate. However, over millions of years, their movements have completely changed the face of our planet.

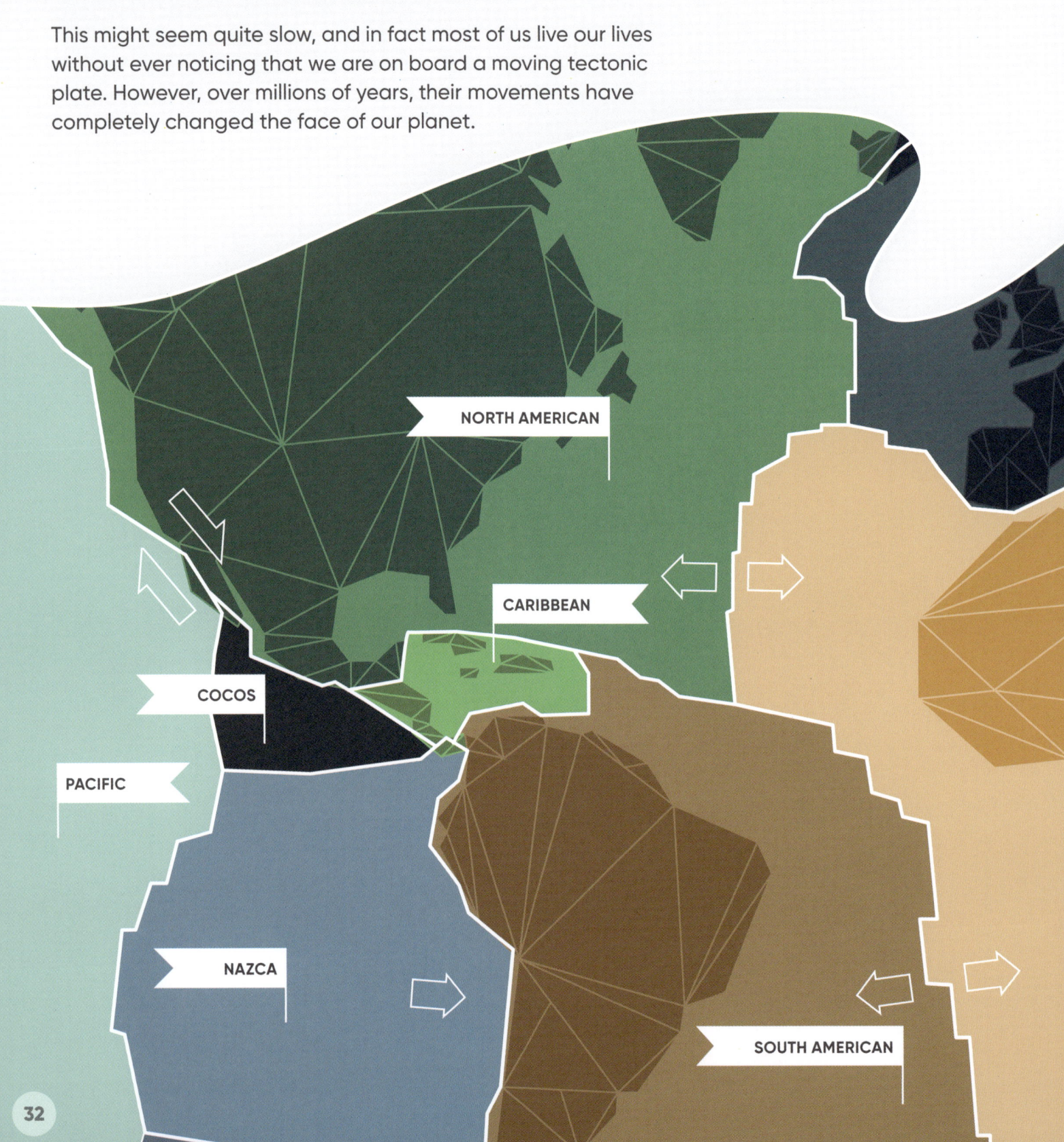

As they move, tectonic plates travel around the surface of Earth, interacting with one another where they meet. Their shapes and sizes change as a result of these interactions, with some plates becoming bigger or smaller over time. Sometimes, completely new plates get created, whilst others get pushed down into Earth's interior, disappearing completely!

This diagram shows most of the tectonic plates on Earth, and the directions they are moving in.

EURASIAN
ARABIAN
PHILIPPINE SEA
INDIAN
PACIFIC
AFRICAN
AUSTRALIAN
ANTARCTIC

# COMING THROUGH!

**Plate boundaries where two tectonic plates are moving past one another are known as conservative boundaries. Along them, lithosphere is neither created nor destroyed.**

A place where this is happening today is the western edge of the North American continent. The boundary between the North American and Pacific plates is a conservative plate boundary.

NORTH AMERICAN PLATE

PACIFIC PLATE

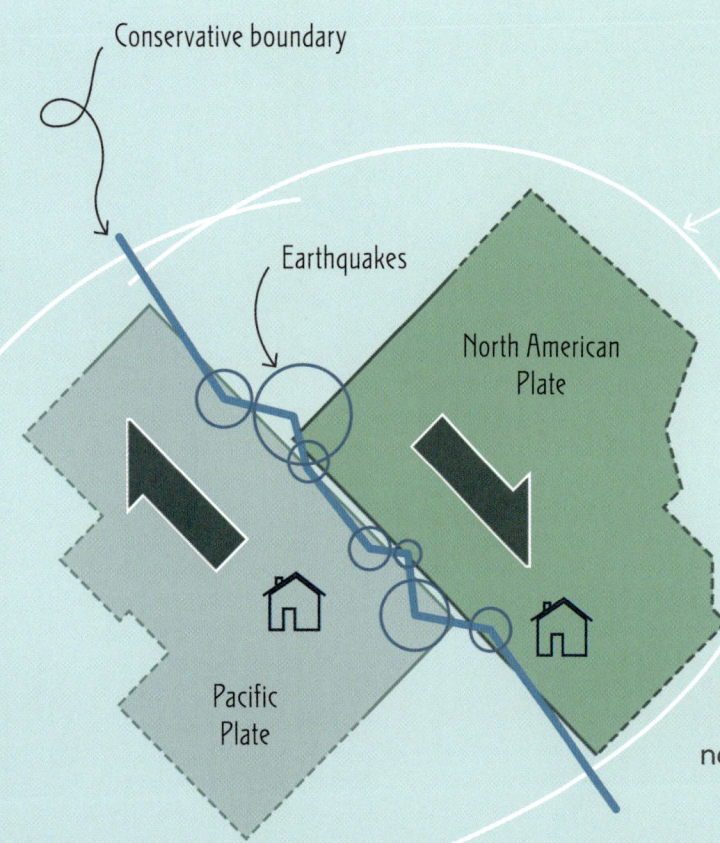

Conservative boundary

Earthquakes

North American Plate

Pacific Plate

If two neighbours lived either side of this type of plate boundary, every year that passed, their houses would become a few inches further apart. Eventually, they would be so far from each other that they wouldn't see each other as neighbours anymore!

However, living so close to places like this comes with some consequences. As plates move past each other, their edges grind and rub, like two cars scraping past each other in a street. This results in lots of earthquakes along their boundary.

People who live along the western coast of North America often experience strong earthquakes as a result of the North American and Pacific plates grinding against each other as they move. Some of these earthquakes happen quite near the surface, whilst others start at depths of more than 15 km (9.3 miles), deep within Earth's crust.

# OPENING UP

The boundaries shared by two plates that are moving away from each other, such as the South American and African plates, are called constructive. They get this name because, along them, new lithosphere is constructed (created).

When seen on a map, constructive plate boundaries are not straight or curved, but instead are stepped. They are formed from straight segments of mid-ocean ridge, separated by long faults (fractures in Earth's surface).

As the African and South American plates move apart, the small gap that opens between them is filled with very hot, partly molten rocks rising from Earth's mantle. When they make contact with sea water, they cool down and become fused (joined) to the existing plates. As this process repeats over time, the plates become bigger, and the ocean becomes wider.

Remember Marie Tharp's underwater mountains? They are actually a chain of volcanoes created by a constructive plate boundary called a mid-ocean ridge.

This is how oceans form on Earth – a plate breaks up, its fragments separate, and new strips of oceanic lithosphere form between them over time.

Partly molten mantle rocks fill the gap between the separating plates.

In contact with cold sea water, the molten rocks solidify and fuse to the plates, so the plates grow in size.

Crust

Lithosphere

Asthenosphere

# ONE BIG PUZZLE

South America and Africa broke apart and started drifting away from each other around 135 million years ago. Before that, they were part of a supercontinent called Pangaea. This huge landmass, made up of all today's continents, occupied almost half of Earth's surface. It was surrounded by the Panthalassan Ocean – a single huge body of water covering the rest of the planet.

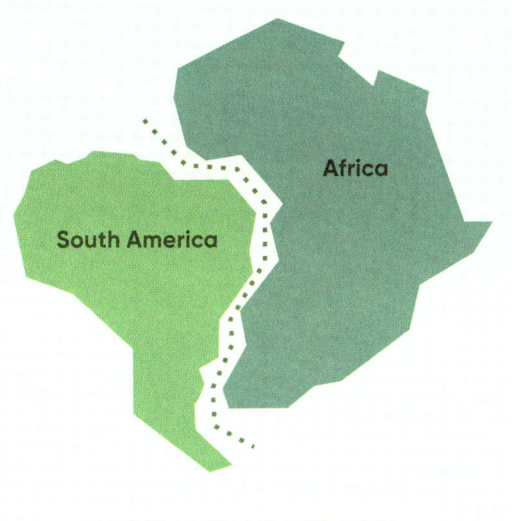

No wonder South America and Africa look like pieces of a puzzle — they are exactly that!

130 MILLION YEARS AGO

80 MILLION YEARS AGO

TODAY

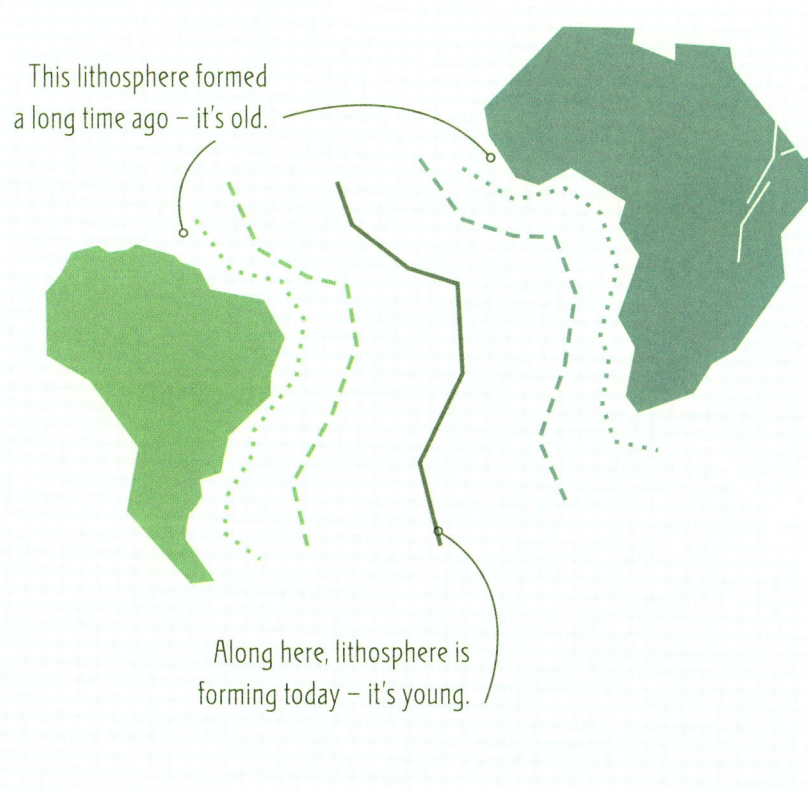

This lithosphere formed a long time ago — it's old.

Along here, lithosphere is forming today — it's young.

TOMORROW…?

# HISTORY REPEATING

Today, volcanoes and earthquakes cluster along the eastern side of the African continent, in and around a great number of very large fractures (faults). These fractures extend for hundreds of kilometres. In fact, some are so big that they can be seen from space.

All of these things tell us that the African Plate has now started rifting (breaking) into two pieces, much the same as Pangaea did millions of years ago. Earth scientists often use this part of the world to collect observations and measurements to investigate how and why tectonic plates break apart.

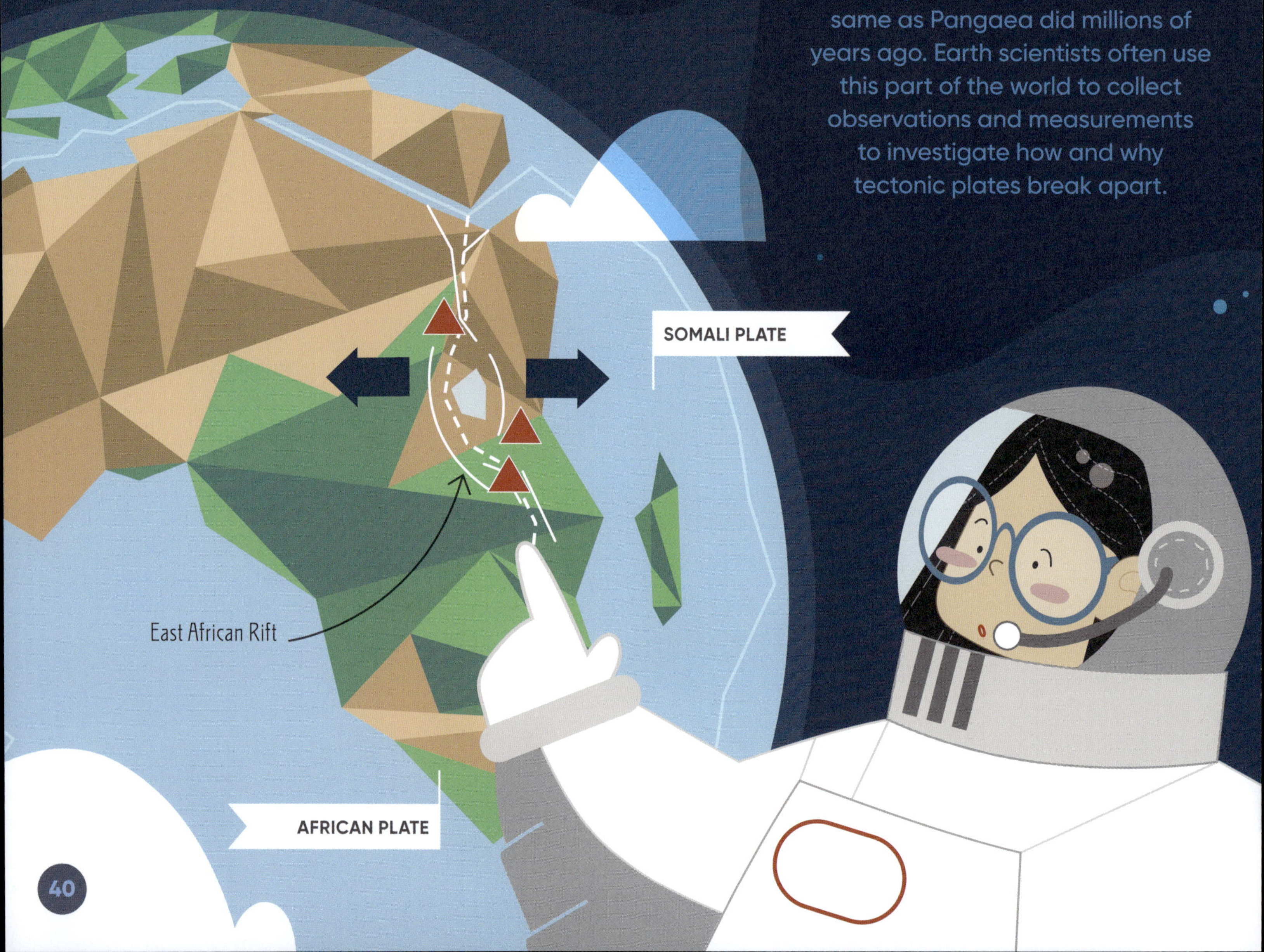

East African Rift

SOMALI PLATE

AFRICAN PLATE

# Constructive or conservative?

Earthquakes and volcanoes are Earth's way of telling us about its restless nature. If you learn how to read them, you can actually figure out the type of boundary between two plates just from the characteristics and amount of earthquakes and volcanoes happening along it!

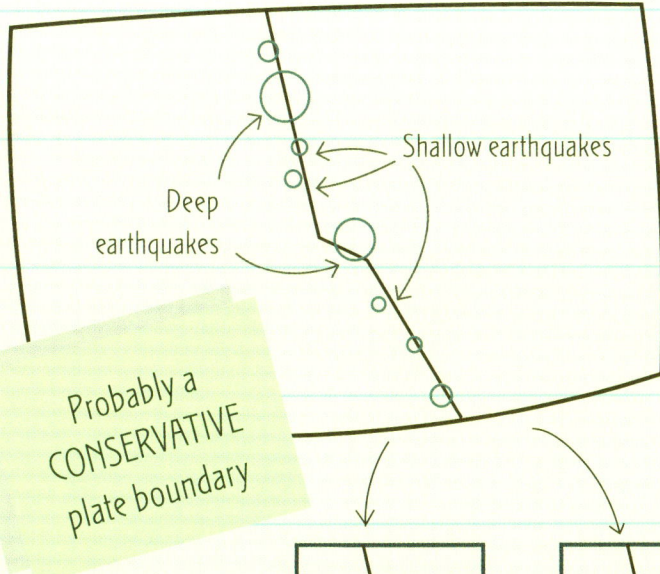

☑ Earthquakes
☒ Volcanoes

It is possible to draw the shape of conservative boundaries by "joining the dots" using earthquake locations.

Some earthquakes happen close to the surface, but others happen deep in Earth's crust.

But there is no way to know which direction plates are moving from earthquake locations alone.

Earthquakes ☑
Volcanoes ☑

Lines of earthquakes also appear along constructive boundaries, but they only happen close to the surface.

Along with earthquakes, the presence of lots of volcanic activity along a narrow band is a strong clue that you are looking at a constructive plate boundary.

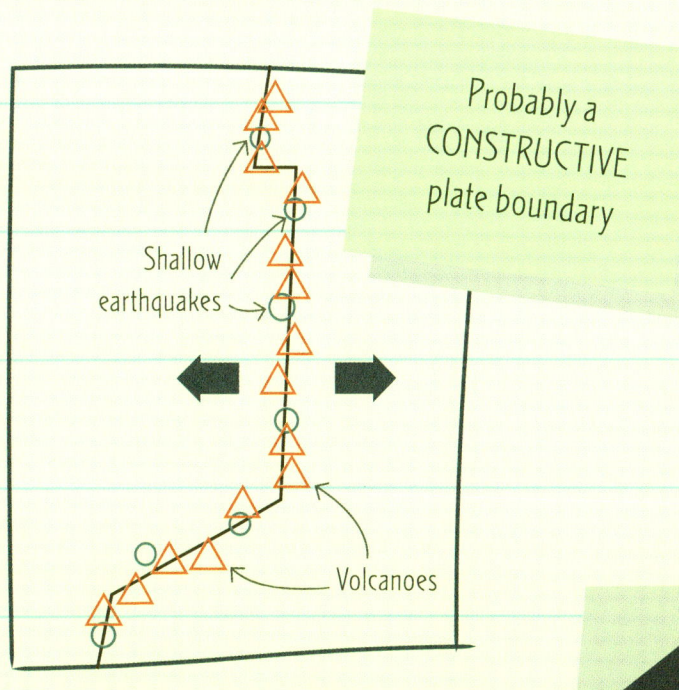

Probably a CONSTRUCTIVE plate boundary

# MAKING SPACE

The trouble with moving plates is that Earth isn't getting any bigger. Plates can't just move away from each other and keep growing and growing forever... there simply isn't any space.

The South American and African plates have been separating for around 135 million years. All of the oceanic lithosphere between the continents has formed over this time.

SOUTH AMERICAN PLATE

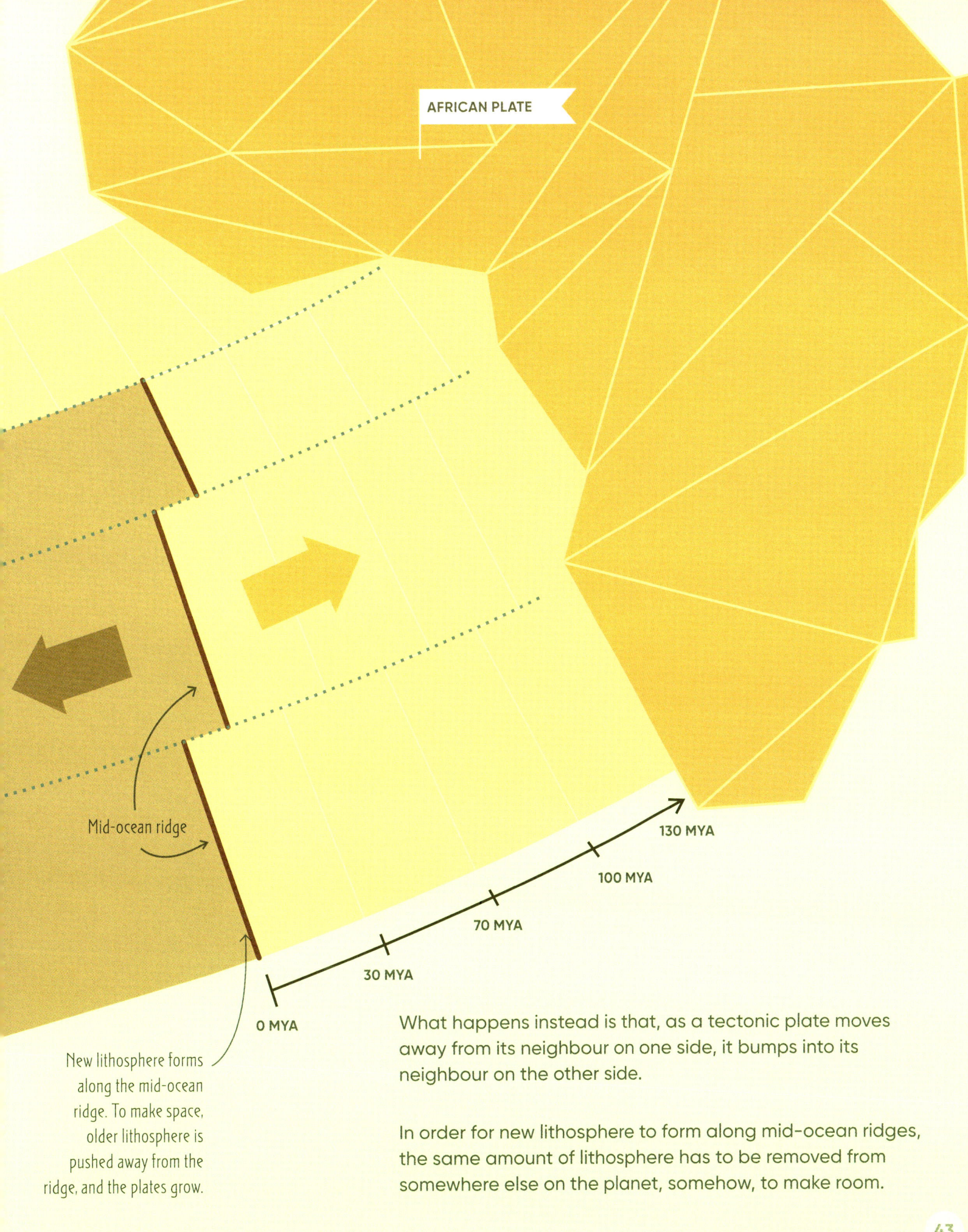

AFRICAN PLATE

Mid-ocean ridge

0 MYA
30 MYA
70 MYA
100 MYA
130 MYA

New lithosphere forms along the mid-ocean ridge. To make space, older lithosphere is pushed away from the ridge, and the plates grow.

What happens instead is that, as a tectonic plate moves away from its neighbour on one side, it bumps into its neighbour on the other side.

In order for new lithosphere to form along mid-ocean ridges, the same amount of lithosphere has to be removed from somewhere else on the planet, somehow, to make room.

# SINKING PLATES

**When two plates collide with each other, the boundary between the two plates is known as destructive. This is because lithosphere (formed by the crust, and the very top of the mantle) is destroyed along it.**

There are a few different ways to destroy lithosphere. Exactly how this is done, and what destructive boundaries look like, depends on the type of lithosphere that is colliding along them.

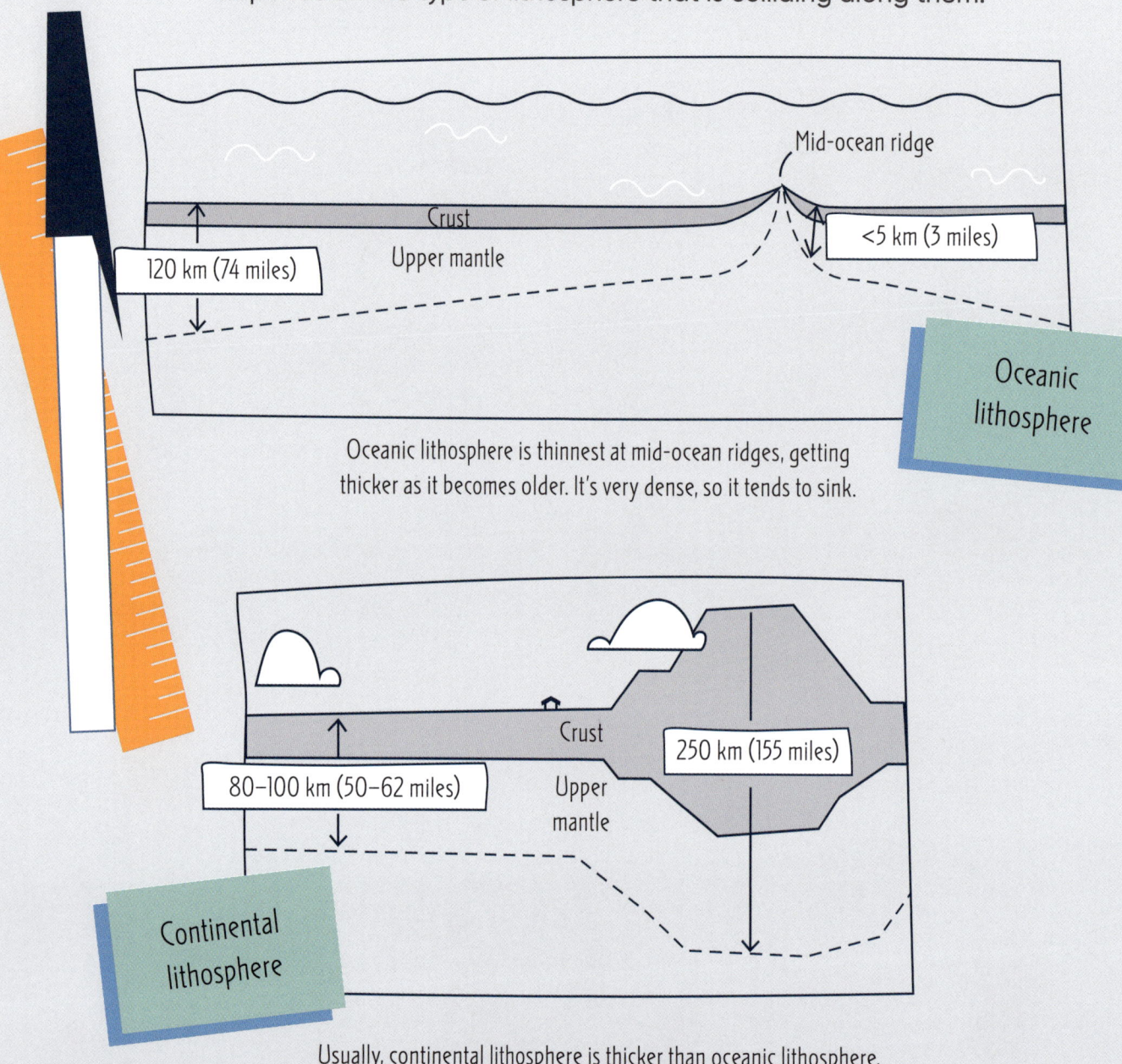

Oceanic lithosphere is thinnest at mid-ocean ridges, getting thicker as it becomes older. It's very dense, so it tends to sink.

Usually, continental lithosphere is thicker than oceanic lithosphere, reaching thicknesses of more than 250 km (155 miles) at the tallest mountain ranges. It is less dense than oceanic lithosphere, so it tends to float.

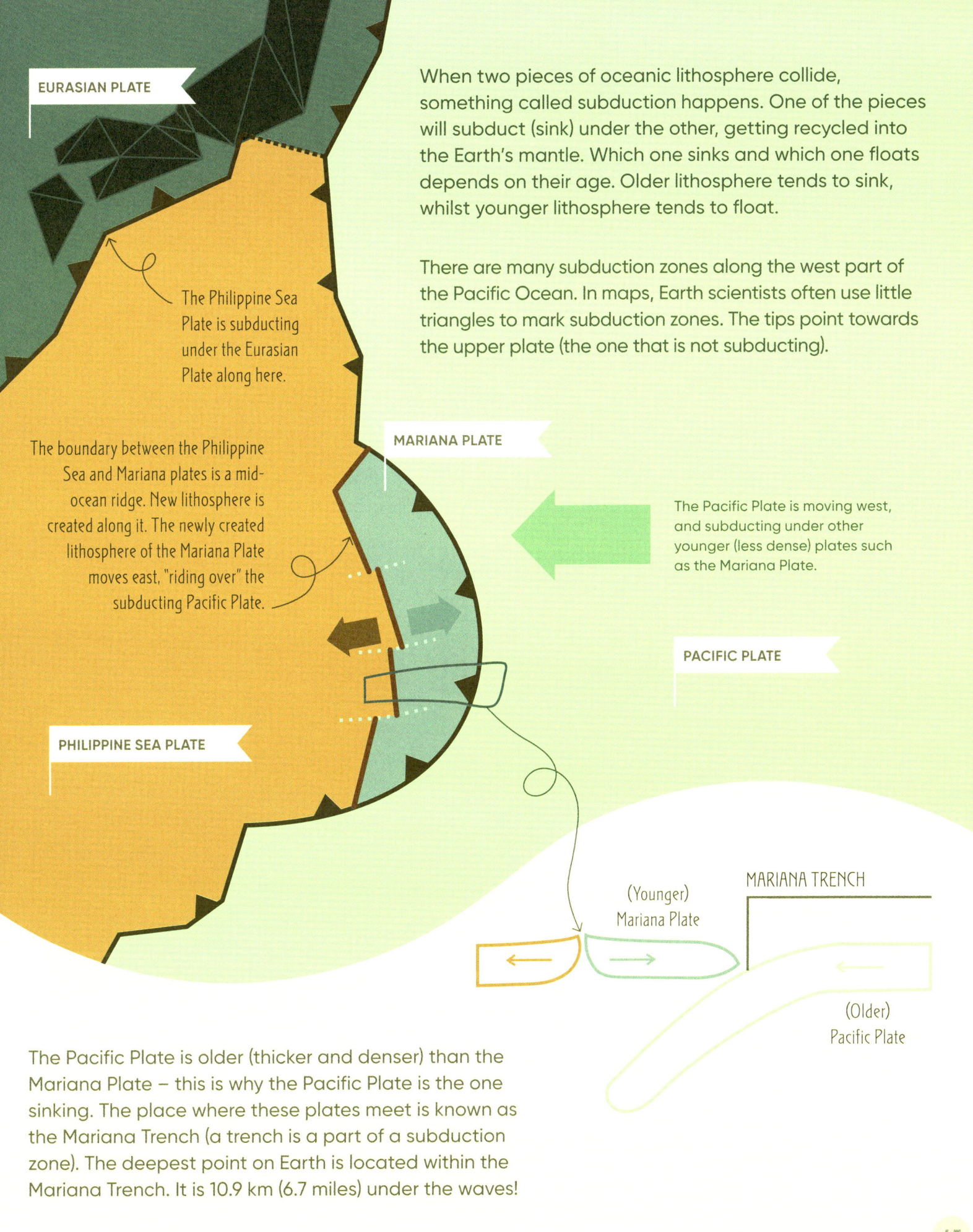

EURASIAN PLATE

When two pieces of oceanic lithosphere collide, something called subduction happens. One of the pieces will subduct (sink) under the other, getting recycled into the Earth's mantle. Which one sinks and which one floats depends on their age. Older lithosphere tends to sink, whilst younger lithosphere tends to float.

There are many subduction zones along the west part of the Pacific Ocean. In maps, Earth scientists often use little triangles to mark subduction zones. The tips point towards the upper plate (the one that is not subducting).

The Philippine Sea Plate is subducting under the Eurasian Plate along here.

MARIANA PLATE

The boundary between the Philippine Sea and Mariana plates is a mid-ocean ridge. New lithosphere is created along it. The newly created lithosphere of the Mariana Plate moves east, "riding over" the subducting Pacific Plate.

The Pacific Plate is moving west, and subducting under other younger (less dense) plates such as the Mariana Plate.

PACIFIC PLATE

PHILIPPINE SEA PLATE

(Younger) Mariana Plate

MARIANA TRENCH

(Older) Pacific Plate

The Pacific Plate is older (thicker and denser) than the Mariana Plate – this is why the Pacific Plate is the one sinking. The place where these plates meet is known as the Mariana Trench (a trench is a part of a subduction zone). The deepest point on Earth is located within the Mariana Trench. It is 10.9 km (6.7 miles) under the waves!

# MORE SINKING PLATES

When oceanic lithosphere and continental lithosphere collide, it is always oceanic lithosphere that subducts. This is because the granite rocks forming continental crust (the top part of the lithosphere) are lighter, and have a tendency to float.

One place where continent-ocean subduction is happening today is along the western edge of South America.

Molten rocks rise up from the mantle, resulting in intense volcanic activity along the upper plate.

The oceanic lithosphere subducts

The continental lithosphere floats

The water contained in rocks and sediments is carried into the mantle as the slab sinks. This water makes it easier for the mantle to melt.

It's not that easy to push a tectonic plate into Earth's interior! Because of that, subduction is accompanied by lots of earthquakes. Scientists can use their depths to "see" the shape of the sinking plate as it disappears into the mantle.

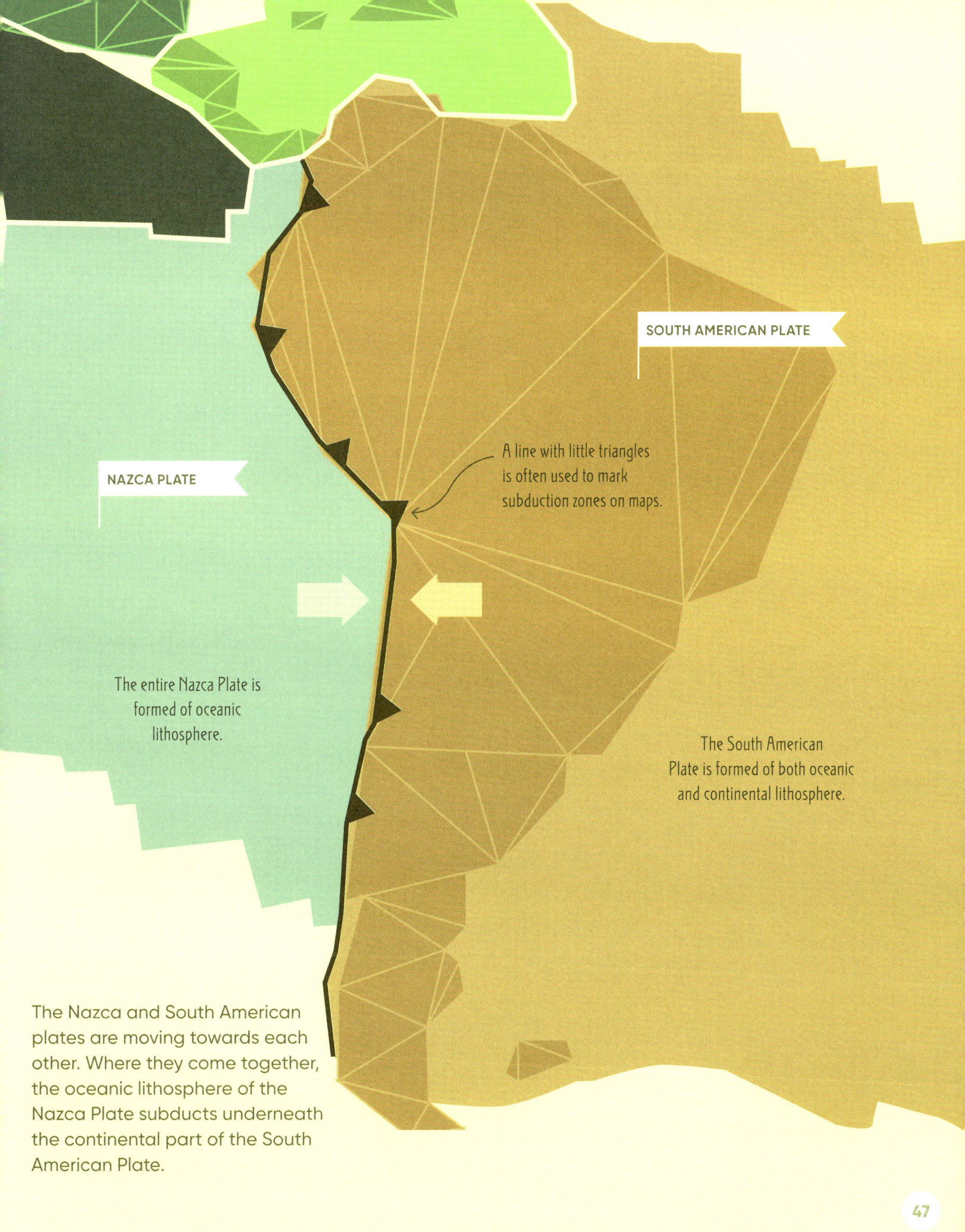

# CRUMPLING PLATES UP

**Unlike continent-ocean collisions, continent-continent collisions don't result in subduction. Instead, the continental lithosphere of the colliding plates pushes together until it crumples up... into mountains!**

This is because, compared to oceanic lithosphere, the rocks forming continental lithosphere are less dense (they are lighter and they tend to float), so making them sink into the mantle is very difficult. It's a bit like trying to push a floating rubber duck underwater in your bath!

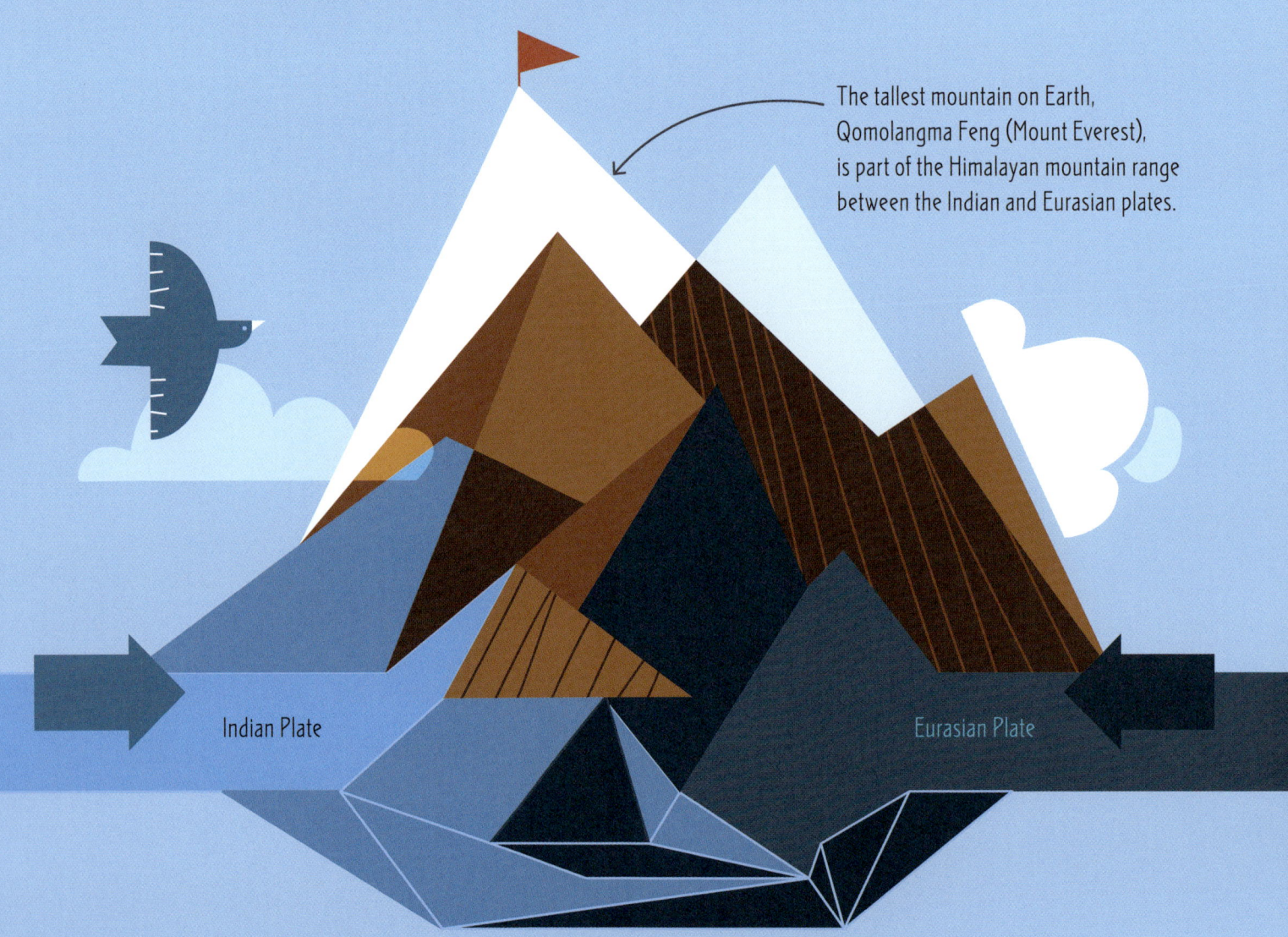

The tallest mountain on Earth, Qomolangma Feng (Mount Everest), is part of the Himalayan mountain range between the Indian and Eurasian plates.

Indian Plate

Eurasian Plate

For the last 50 million years or so, the Indian Plate has been colliding with the Eurasian Plate – this is how the Himalayan mountain range has formed! The mountains get a little bit taller every year as the plates continue to push together.

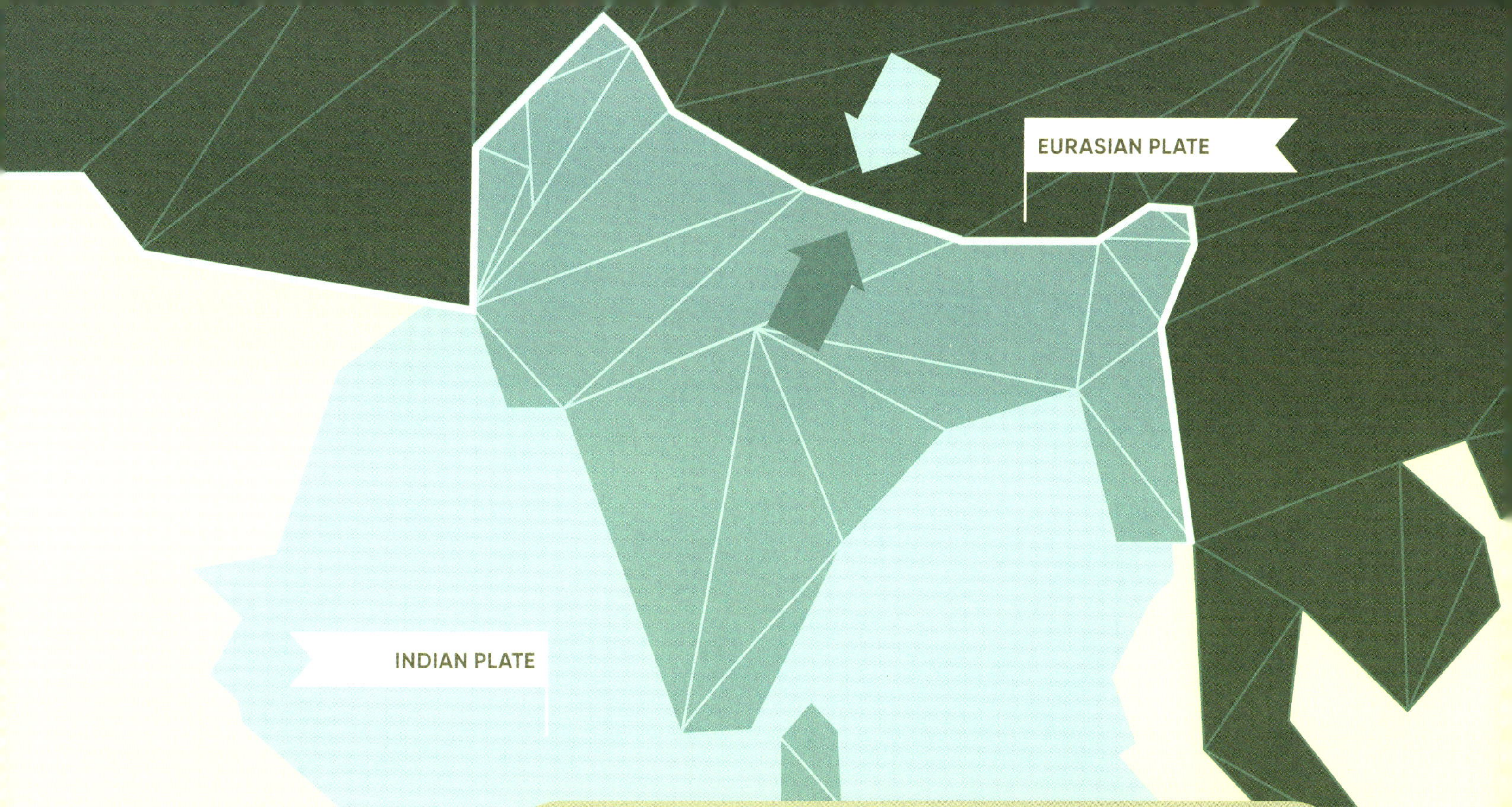

**EURASIAN PLATE**

**INDIAN PLATE**

## Subducting or colliding?

**Subduction zones**

☑ Earthquakes
☑ Volcanoes

Subduction zones (where one plate sinks under another) experience lots of earthquakes. The earthquakes happen at shallow depths when they are close to the plate boundary, and get deeper the further they are away from it (because they are caused by the sinking slab). There is also volcanic activity, but only on the non-subducting plate (the upper plate).

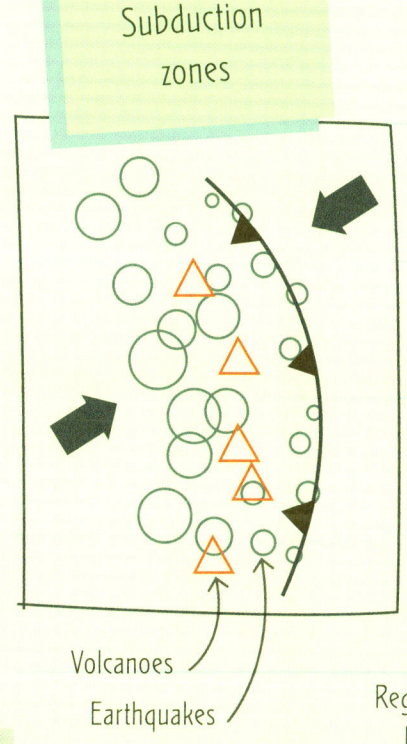

Volcanoes
Earthquakes

**Continental collision**

Earthquakes ☑
Volcanoes ☒

Regions where plates are colliding also experience lots of earthquakes over very wide areas, in and around the plate boundary, but no volcanoes.

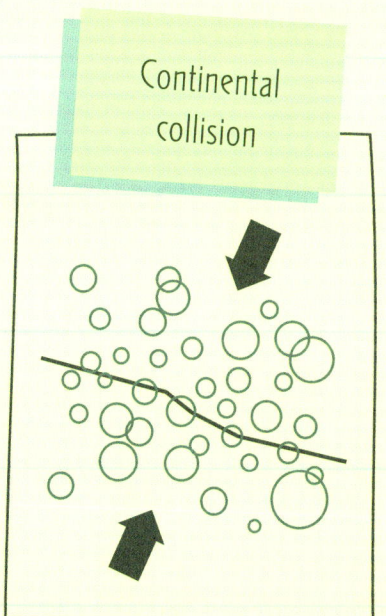

49

# AN INTERCONNECTED SYSTEM

Over millions of years, lithosphere that formed at mid-ocean ridges moved across the surface of the planet, before eventually being recycled back into the mantle by subduction.

For a long time, scientists wondered what drove tectonic plates. It almost seemed as if, under the surface of Earth, there was a complex system of gears and conveyor belts, all powered by a mysterious engine hidden within the interior of the planet.

# WHAT DRIVES PLATE TECTONICS?

**What is the engine that keeps tectonic plates moving?**

For quite some time, Earth scientists thought something called convection currents in the mantle kept tectonic plates moving. You can think of convection currents a little bit like huge, loop-shaped conveyor belts pushing and pulling on the underside of tectonic plates.

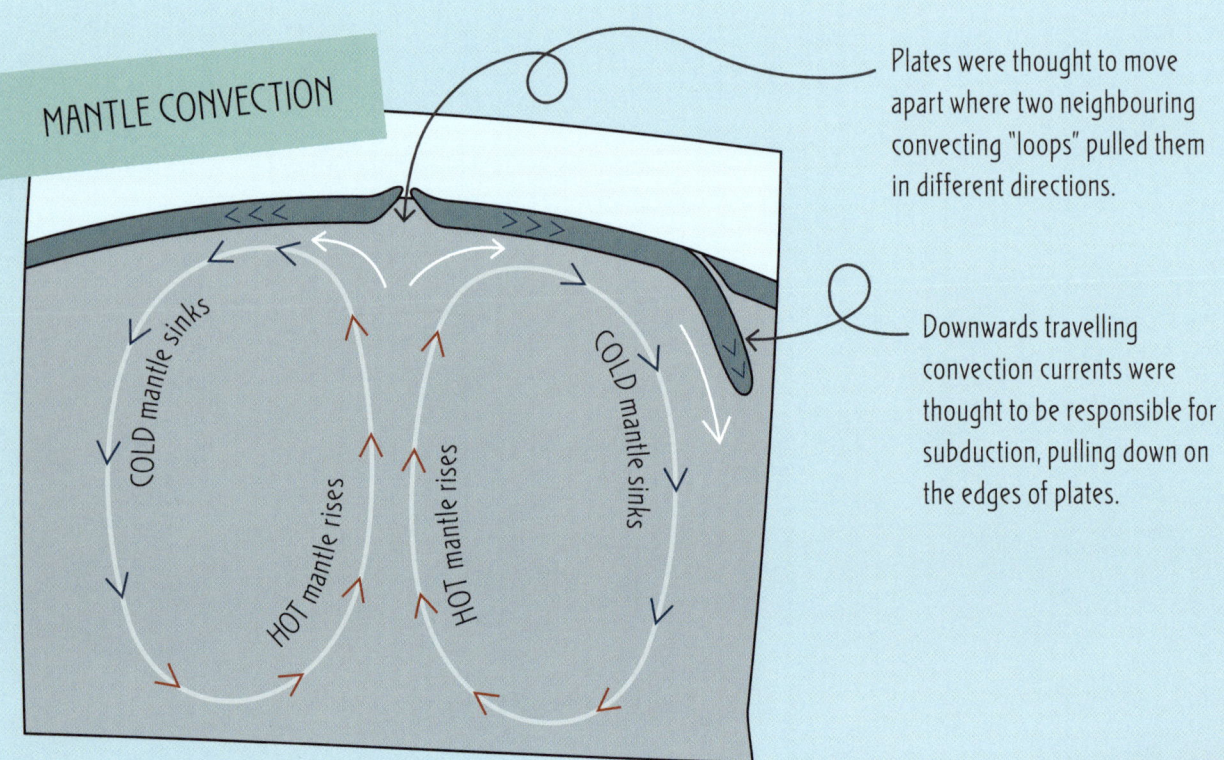

Plates were thought to move apart where two neighbouring convecting "loops" pulled them in different directions.

Downwards travelling convection currents were thought to be responsible for subduction, pulling down on the edges of plates.

The Earth's mantle has currents because not all of it is the same temperature. Hot mantle, found nearer the Earth's core, tends to rise so it moves upwards. As it gets closer to the surface, it cools a bit, which causes it to begin sinking back down. Near the core, it warms up again, and rises, so the cycle repeats.

However, eventually scientists have realized that the forces created by these currents are not very strong. By themselves, it seems unlikely that they could move huge chunks of lithosphere around.

Today, Earth scientists think instead that the key to understanding the motions of tectonic plates may be hidden in subduction zones. Subducting slabs, the sinking portions of tectonic plates, are heavy! Once they start sinking, they generate huge pulling forces, dragging the rest of the tectonic plate along with them.

"Slab pull" forces are thought to be the main drivers of plate tectonics. How strongly a sinking slab can pull down a plate depends on its size - larger slabs generate larger pull forces.

Convection currents in the mantle do exist, but they don't affect the movement of tectonic plates as much as was originally thought.

# ONE WORLD TODAY

The fact that tectonic plates are constantly moving means that the face of Earth is changing every single day. But because most plates move very, very slowly, the changes are not all that obvious within a person's lifetime.

### AMASIA
Because there are several plates currently moving north, it is possible they could end up forming a supercontinent at the planet's North Pole. This possible supercontinent has been named "Amasia".

### AURICA
Another possibility is that both the Atlantic and Pacific oceans will close. The continents around them will then come together to form "Aurica".

### PANGAEA ULTIMA
Perhaps only the Atlantic will close, and the continents either side of it will collide again. It would look a bit like the supercontinent Pangaea did 250 million years ago, but this time, the continents would form a ring shape with a small ocean in the middle.

**NOVOPANGAEA**

It is most likely that the Pacific Ocean, which is already shrinking, will continue to shrink. The continents around it would come together if it eventually disappears completely.

# A DIFFERENT WORLD TOMORROW

If you travelled a couple of hundred million years into the future, you would find that the world looked very different! What exactly it would look like is hard to predict, but it would depend strongly on which parts of today's tectonic plates have sunk. Here are some ideas about what could happen.

# PUTTING THE PIECES TOGETHER

Once the puzzle is complete, it is easy to see where every piece fits. Earthquakes and volcanoes, underwater mountain ranges, the shapes of our continents today... they can all be explained by one single theory – plate tectonics.

### CONSERVATIVE plate boundaries

- ✗ Volcanoes
- ✓ Earthquakes – they can be shallow or deep, and occur aligned along a narrow ribbon

Some continents look like they once fitted together because they did! Then they broke into pieces, each moving away as part of a different plate.

### CONSTRUCTIVE plate boundaries

- ✓ Volcanoes – the chain of underwater mountains discovered by Marie Tharp is a chain of volcanoes!
- ✓ Earthquakes – not many; they originate close to the surface and appear along a narrow ribbon marking the plate boundary

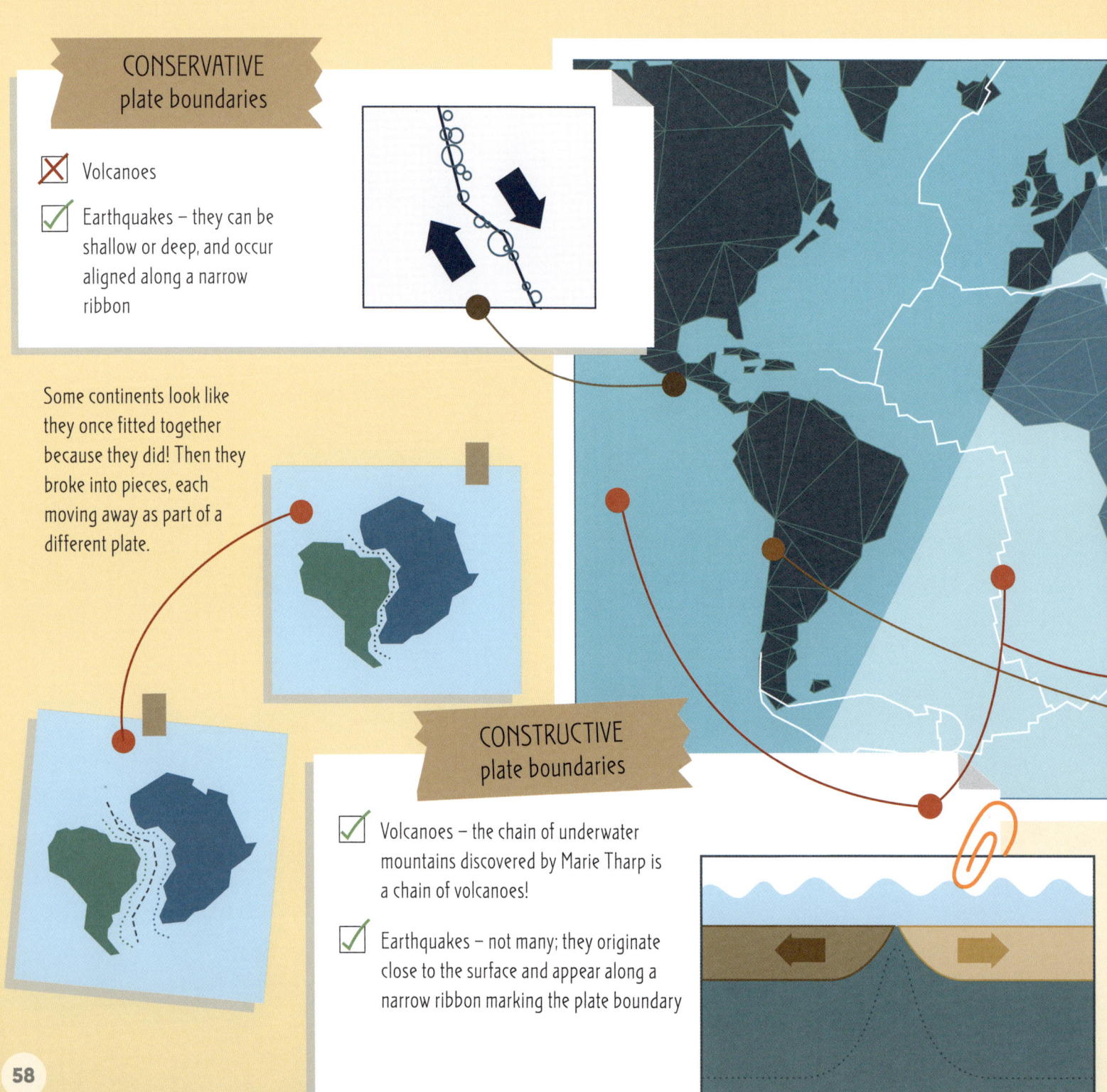

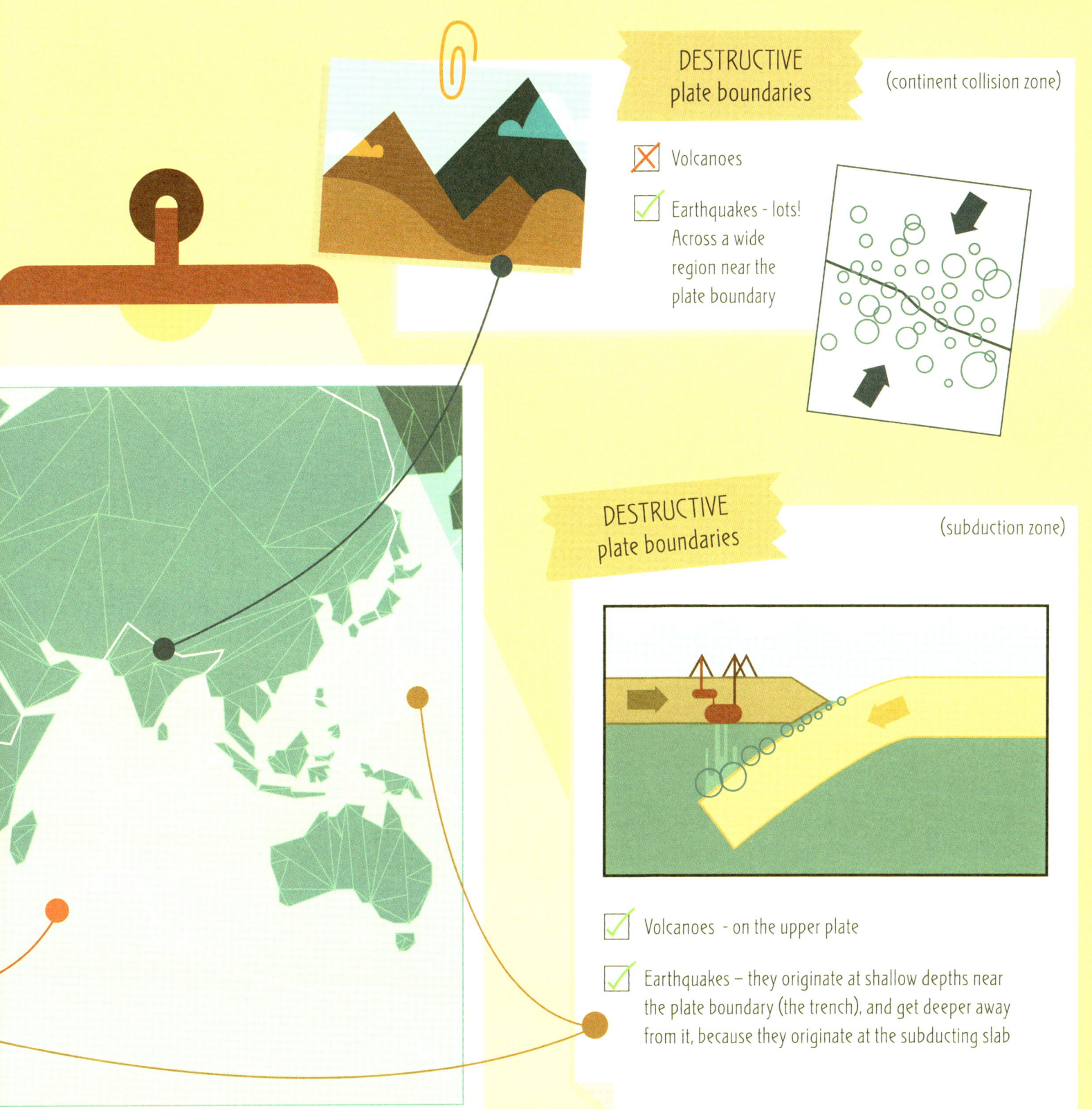

## DESTRUCTIVE plate boundaries (continent collision zone)

☒ Volcanoes

☑ Earthquakes - lots! Across a wide region near the plate boundary

## DESTRUCTIVE plate boundaries (subduction zone)

☑ Volcanoes - on the upper plate

☑ Earthquakes – they originate at shallow depths near the plate boundary (the trench), and get deeper away from it, because they originate at the subducting slab

Plate tectonics explains the wonderful variety of landscapes that we see on Earth – which are the source of so many resources that support life. But its significance for the existence of life on our planet goes much further than that.

In fact, without plate tectonics, we **may not be here at all**.

# THE SECRET INGREDIENT FOR LIFE

One of the most important ingredients for the existence of life on any planet is water – lots of it, and in liquid form. If you are a rock floating in space, holding on to liquid water is not easy! If temperatures are too cold, like on Mars, water will turn into ice. If they are too warm, like on Venus or Mercury, water will evaporate and be lost to space. Either way, any form of life will die.

So why was Earth, unlike its neighbours, able to hold on to lots of liquid water?

Because of **plate tectonics**.

Earth's atmosphere contains oxygen for life to breathe, as well as gases that control how much heat our planet can hold on to – they are called greenhouse gases.

Without these gases in its atmosphere, Earth would get too cold. But if they build up too much, Earth will get too warm. Plate tectonics has helped maintain the balance of gases in Earth's atmosphere for billions of years, because while some tectonic processes create greenhouse gases, others recycle them.

This balance of gases in Earth's atmosphere is delicate. Even small changes to the amounts of different gases in the atmosphere can have a really big impact on whether life can exist on our planet.

Greenhouse gases, such as carbon dioxide, trap heat. When there is too much of them in a planet's atmosphere, the planet becomes a rather toasty place, just like a greenhouse in the summer!

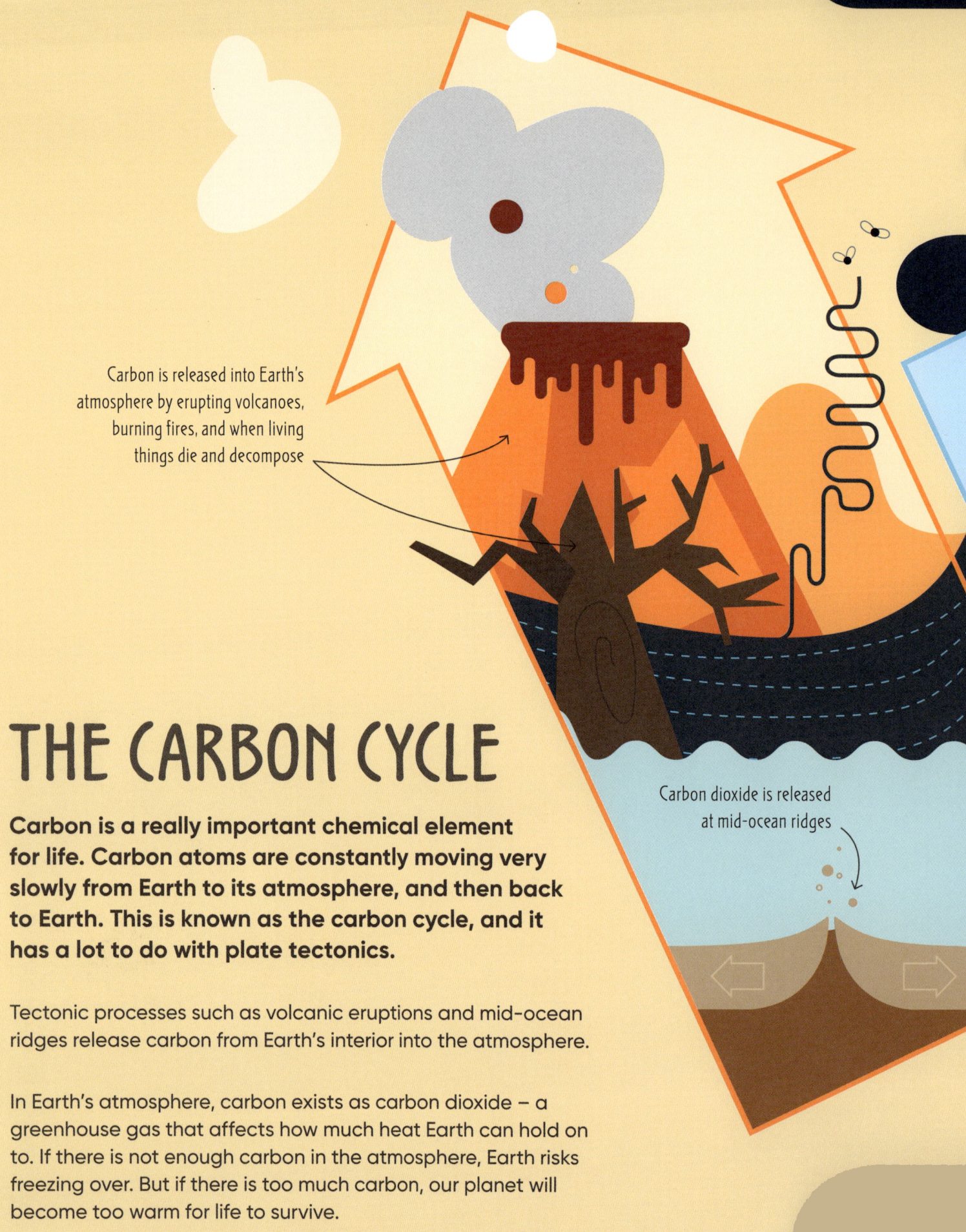

Carbon is released into Earth's atmosphere by erupting volcanoes, burning fires, and when living things die and decompose

Carbon dioxide is released at mid-ocean ridges

# THE CARBON CYCLE

**Carbon is a really important chemical element for life. Carbon atoms are constantly moving very slowly from Earth to its atmosphere, and then back to Earth. This is known as the carbon cycle, and it has a lot to do with plate tectonics.**

Tectonic processes such as volcanic eruptions and mid-ocean ridges release carbon from Earth's interior into the atmosphere.

In Earth's atmosphere, carbon exists as carbon dioxide – a greenhouse gas that affects how much heat Earth can hold on to. If there is not enough carbon in the atmosphere, Earth risks freezing over. But if there is too much carbon, our planet will become too warm for life to survive.

Bringing carbon from the atmosphere back to Earth's interior takes quite a few steps, some of which rely on plate tectonics too. The carbon first needs to get back to Earth's surface (for example, carried by rainwater). There, through a series of chemical reactions, it gets trapped into rocks that are returned into the mantle by subduction.

Earth and its atmosphere are a closed system. No new carbon is added to this system from the Universe. For this reason, the total amount of carbon has remained the same throughout Earth's life – carbon simply moves around in a cycle, over and over again.

Some carbon is absorbed by plant and plankton photosynthesis, and by the oceans

Some carbon gets locked in rocks and subducted into the mantle

# MOVING TOO FAST

Plate tectonics has enabled life to exist on Earth for billions of years, through controlling things such as the amount of greenhouse gases in the atmosphere. However, this delicate balance is at risk because of us – humans.

Deforestation

Cattle farming

# TIME TO ACT!

We are adding carbon to the atmosphere a lot faster than Earth can recycle it back into the planet's interior. This means that carbon builds up in the atmosphere. As the amount of carbon grows over time, Earth's temperature increases. This is happening too fast for most animal and plant species to adapt to the change – us included.

In a year, it is estimated that all of the thousands of volcanoes on planet Earth collectively pump between 130-400 million metric tonnes (145-448 million tons) of carbon dioxide into the atmosphere.

Annual human emissions of carbon dioxide are more than 60 times greater.

The good news is, it's in **our hands to change this.**

# NOT JUST OUR PLANET

**The choices we make in our daily lives can affect the impact we have on the planet. There are lots of little things we can all do to live more sustainably – from thinking about how much water and energy we use to choosing transport that produces less pollution.**

By only using the resources that we need, we can reduce our environmental impact and help Earth stay in balance... not just for humans to keep living in it, but also for all other life.

Take showers instead of baths

Choose reusable materials instead of single-use ones

Use rainwater to water your plants

Reduce how much meat and dairy you eat

Recycle and reduce (consume less!)

Walk or cycle instead of driving

Turn off lights when not using them

**Bacteria** 12.83%

**Fungi** 2.20%

**Protists** 0.73%

**Plants** 82.45%
(of all life forms on Earth)

**Archaea** 1.28%

Viruses 0.04%  Humans

Animals 0.47%

**Humans,** making up only around 0.18 per cent of all animals, are a really small proportion of all life on Earth! In this diagram, we can be **represented by a tiny dot**!

Archaea and protists are tiny single-cell organisms

# WORLDS TO DISCOVER

Plate tectonics plays such an important role in creating and maintaining a liveable planet. The more we learn about it, the more likely it is that we will be able to understand whether other planets or moons with solid surfaces could have life too.

But there is **a lot** that we still don't know.

# WHY?

# WHEN?

When Earth formed, it was an incandescent ball of molten rock, too hot for a rigid lithosphere or the plate tectonics that comes with one. So when exactly did plate tectonics start? What caused the lithosphere to break into tectonic plates? What is the engine that started the plates' movements?

The answers to these questions are still to be found...

# HOW?

# A GROUP EFFORT

Solving these mysteries requires many of us to work together, searching for clues within Earth's geological record until we are able to explain how the clues fit together.

Only then will we be able to write the **next chapter of this story**

Will you join us?

# GLOSSARY

**ARID**
very dry

**ASTEROID**
chunk of rock that orbits the Sun

**ASTHENOSPHERE**
part of the mantle found directly below the lithosphere

**ATMOSPHERE**
layer of gases surrounding a planet

**BOUNDARY**
place where one tectonic plate meets another tectonic plate

**CHEMICAL ELEMENT**
one of 118 substances that make up all known materials

**CHEMICAL REACTION**
event in which two substances combine to form a new one, sometimes releasing heat or light in the process

**CONSERVATIVE BOUNDARY**
boundary where two tectonic plates are moving alongside each other and many earthquakes occur

**CONSTRUCTIVE BOUNDARY**
boundary where two tectonic plates are moving apart and new rock is being created

**CONTINENT**
one of seven very large areas that the Earth's land is divided into, such as South America, or Europe

**CONTINENTAL**
relating to continents

**CORE**
central layer of the Earth

**COSMIC RADIATION**
flow of harmful particles from space, many of which are blocked by Earth's atmosphere

**CRUST**
top layer of the Earth, made of solid rock

**DECOMPOSE**
rot

**DEFORESTATION**
chopping down trees and destroying forests so there are none left in an area

**DENSE**
description of a substance that has its particles packed tightly together making it heavy

**DESTRUCTIVE BOUNDARY**
boundary where two tectonic plates are colliding. At this type of boundary, either one plate sinks beneath (is subducted under) the other or both plate edges are pushed together to form mountains

**EARTHQUAKE**
when the ground shakes because of movements in the Earth's crust

**FAULT**
surface that separates two blocks of rock (or two pieces of crust) that are moving with respect to each other

**FOSSIL**
remains of a dead animal or plant that have been preserved in rock

**FOSSIL FUELS**
fuels made from the remains of animals and plants that died millions of years ago, such as oil and coal

**GREENHOUSE GASES**
gases in the atmosphere that trap heat from the Sun

**HORN OF AFRICA**
easternmost part of Africa that sticks out into the Indian Ocean

**INCANDESCENT**
when something is glowing because it is very hot

**LITHOSPHERE**
outer layer of the Earth made up of the crust and the top of the mantle. The lithosphere is broken into tectonic plates

**MAGNETIC FIELD**
area of magnetism surrounding a magnet or a planetary body

**MANTLE**
layer of Earth between the crust and the core. It is made of extremely hot rock and although it is solid, it can flow very slowly

**MID-OCEAN RIDGE**
underwater chain of volcanoes found along constructive plate boundaries

**MOON**
large, often round, chunk of rock that orbits a planet

**OCEANIC**
relating to oceans

**ORBIT**
when one object in space circles around another

**PANGAEA**
supercontinent that existed millions of years ago

**PHOTOSYNTHESIS**
process by which plants and plankton make food (sugar) from carbon dioxide and water using energy from the Sun

**PLANET**
large, round object that orbits a star. Planets can be made of rock or gas

**PLATE TECTONICS**
process by which the Earth's tectonic plates move around

**POLLUTION**
gases, chemicals, or objects that damage the planet

**RIFTING**
breaking apart of a tectonic plate

**RING OF FIRE**
line around the Pacific Plate where most of the world's volcanoes are found

**SEISMOGRAPH**
device used to measure earthquakes

**SOLAR SYSTEM**
the Sun and all the objects that orbit it, including the planets

**SOLAR WINDS**
flow of particles from the Sun

**SONAR**
technology that uses sound and echoes to measure distances

**SUBDUCTION**
when the edge of one tectonic plate sinks beneath another plate

**SUPERCONTINENT**
huge area of land that covers a large part of the Earth

**SUSTAINABLE**
able to continue for a long time without damaging the planet

**TECTONIC PLATE**
one of many large pieces of the Earth's lithosphere

**UNIVERSE**
all of space

**VOLCANO**
opening in the Earth's crust, usually in the shape of a mountain, out of which lava and gas erupt from the mantle below

# INDEX

## A
Africa 23, 38–39, 55
African Plate 36–37, 42–43, 55
Amasia 56
animals 69
Antarctic Plate 33
Arabian Plate 33
archaea 69
Asia 23
  see also Eurasian Plate
asthenosphere 27, 28, 31
Atlantic Ocean 20–21, 56
atmosphere 11, 26, 61–63
  see also greenhouse gases
Aurica 56
Australian Plate 33, 55

## B
bacteria 69
boreholes 30
boundaries 58–59
  conservative 34–35, 58
  constructive 36–37, 58
  destructive 44–49, 59

## C
carbon cycle 62–63
carbon dioxide 61, 62, 67
Caribbean Plate 32
cartography 20–21
Cocos Plate 32
conservative boundaries 34–35, 58
constructive boundaries 36–37, 58
continental collision 48–49, 59
continental crust 26
continental drift 17, 38–39
continental lithosphere 44, 46–47, 48
continents 16–17, 22–23, 38, 56–57
convection currents 52–53
core 26–27
crust 26, 27

## D
destructive boundaries 44–49, 59

## E
Earth 9, 10–11, 26–27
earthquakes 22–23, 34–35, 46, 49
East African Rift 55
Eurasian Plate 33, 45, 48–49, 55
Europe 23
Everest, Mount (Qomolangma Feng) 30, 48

## F
fossils 17
freshwater 18
fungi 69

## G
gas giants 8
greenhouse gases 61, 62, 64–65

## H
Himalayan Mountains 48, 55
humans 64–65, 67, 68–69

## I
Indian Plate 33, 48–49, 55
inner core 27

## J
Juan de Fuca Plate 54

## K
Kármán line 11

## L
life 11, 12, 69
lithosphere 27, 28–29, 31, 34
  continental 44, 46–47, 48
  oceanic 36–37, 42–43, 44–47

## M
magnetic field 10–11
mantle 26–27, 30–31, 37, 44
mantle convection 52–53
Mariana Plate 45
Mariana Trench 12, 30, 45

Mars 9
Mercury 9
Mid-Atlantic Ridge 54
mid-ocean ridges 36, 42–43, 44, 62
mountain ranges 21, 30, 44, 48
movement 28–29, 32–33, 52, 54 see also boundaries

## N
Nazca Plate 32, 46–47, 54
North America 22, 35
North American Plate 32, 34–35, 54
North Atlantic see Atlantic Ocean
north magnetic pole 10
Novopangaea 57

## O
Oceania 23
oceanic crust 26
oceanic lithosphere 34, 36–37, 42–43, 44–47
oceans 18–21, 30, 37
outer core 27

## P
Pacific Ocean 23, 56, 57
Pacific Plate 32–33, 34–35, 45, 54–55
Pangaea 38–39
Pangaea Ultima 56
Panthalassan Ocean 38
peridotite 27
Philippine Sea Plate 33, 45

plants 69
plate movement 28–29, 32–33, 52, 54 see also boundaries
plate tectonic theory 28–29, 56–57, 70–74
poles 10, 56
protists 69

## Q
Qomolangma Feng (Mount Everest) 30, 48

## R
ridge push 53
Ring of Fire 55
rocky planets 9

## S
seafloor 19, 20–21
seas see oceans
seismographs 22
slab pull 53
Solar System 8–9, 10–11
solar winds 10
sonar 19, 20
sound waves 19
South America 22, 38–39, 54
South American Plate 32, 36–37, 42–43, 46–47
south magnetic pole 10
subduction 45–47, 52, 53, 63
subduction zones 45, 49, 54–55, 59
Sun 8
supercontinent 38, 56
sustainability 68

## T
Tharp, Marie 21, 23, 37

## V
Venus 9
viruses 69
volcanoes 22–23, 46, 49
 in the carbon cycle 62, 67

## W
water 18, 60, 68
Wegener, Alfred 17–19

# ACKNOWLEDGEMENTS

The publisher would like to thank:

Laura Gilbert for proofreading, Elizabeth Wise for the index, Brandie Tully-Scott for design, and Olivia Stanford for editorial.

## From Lucía:

To my wonderful agents Gill and Gatsby - thanks for believing in me and my ideas, and for your support whilst I navigated the labyrinth of publishing my first book. Same goes for my Inkpot Collective family, who have provided a lot of insight and encouragement.

Many people have helped me in creating "How the Earth Works" by reading the drafts, commenting on the illustrations, and patiently allowing me to go on and on about it for what seems like years. In particular, I would like to thank Craig, Eoghan, Fabio, Kirstie, and Sean.

Graeme - I know that finding mistakes I made and correcting them remains one of your favourite things to do, so there was no question I would ask you to sense-check the science content. And you did, whilst elegantly showing me once more that much to my annoyance, you remain the cleverer of the two of us.

Last but certainly not least, I must thank my youngest advisor Magnus. Thank you for the hours of drawing practice you have shared with me, and for looking through the early version of this book and telling me that other 7 year old children would like it for sure.